COUNT IT ALL *Joy*

COUNT IT ALL *Joy*

Discover a Happiness That Circumstances Cannot Change

DR. DAVID JEREMIAH

DAVID **C** COOK™

transforming lives together

COUNT IT ALL JOY
Published by David C Cook
4050 Lee Vance Drive
Colorado Springs, CO 80918 U.S.A.

Integrity Music Limited, a Division of David C Cook
Brighton, East Sussex BN1 2RE, England

The graphic circle C logo is a registered trademark of David C Cook.

Unless otherwise noted, all Scripture quotations are taken from the New King James
Version®. Copyright © 1982 by Thomas Nelson. Used by permission. All rights
reserved. Scripture quotations marked KJV are taken from the King James Version of
the Bible. (Public Domain.); PHILLIPS are taken from The New Testament in Modern
English by J. B. Philips copyright © 1960, 1972 J. B. Phillips. Administered by
The Archbishops' Council of the Church of England. Used by Permission.
Other Scripture quotations are taken from *The Holy Bible: A New Translation*,
© 1922, 1924, 1925, 1926, 1935, by Harper & Row, Publishers, Inc.
© 1950, 1952, 1953, 1954, by James A. R. Moffatt (MOFFATT) and from *Wuest's
Word Studies: Philippians in the Greek New Testament* by Kenneth S. Wuest,
© 1942 by the Wm. B. Eerdmans Publishing Co. Used by permission.
The author has added italics to Scripture quotations for emphasis.

LCCN 2015952816
Hardcover ISBN 978-1-4347-0875-5
Paperback ISBN 978-1-4347-1066-6
eISBN 978-1-4347-1008-6

© 2016 David Jeremiah
Published in association with Yates & Yates, www.yates2.com.
First edition published by Victor Books/SP Publications, Inc. in 1992
© David Jeremiah, ISBN 978-0-7814-4366-1, *Turning Toward Joy*

Readers' Guide prepared by Patricia Picardi. The Team: Alex Field, Ingrid
Beck, Amy Konyndyk, Nick Lee, Tiffany Thomas, Susan Murdock
Cover Design: Jon Middel
Cover Photo: Thinkstock

Printed in the United States of America
Second Edition 2016

4 5 6 7 8 9 10 11 12 13

032119

To Warren Wiersbe
Godly Example, Great Communicator,
Gifted Writer, Good Friend

CONTENTS

ACKNOWLEDGMENTS

As I was finishing this first book in the new Turning Point series, I thought of the many people who had encouraged me in this project. Dr. Merritt Barber, a dentist in our church, has many times expressed to me the hope that someday our Bible study material could be packaged for use in home Bible studies. When you are in a dental chair and your mouth is full of Novocain, you can't do much else but listen. I did!

For the last five years, every time I have seen Victor Books' Mark Sweeney, he has reminded me that we ought to work on such a project together. We finally did it, Mark! Warren Wiersbe, who has given us the wonderful Be series of Bible studies, has urged me often to begin this process. As we shared a meal in Dayton, Tennessee, he finally convinced me that I should make this a priority.

My father, Dr. James T. Jeremiah, has consistently reminded me that writing should be a part of my life. My wife, Donna, has cheered me on when the pressures of our busy life made the completion of this assignment seem impossible. Paul Joiner added a whole new dimension to our study of God's Word through his creative writing and directing of the dramatic sketches that correspond to each lesson. Glenda Parker, my administrative assistant, diligently protected my time for study and writing. My friends around the country tell me she is the best gatekeeper they have ever met! Without her efforts, this book would not be a reality.

As I reflect upon all these wonderful friends, I am drawn to the words Paul used to express his love for the Philippian believers: "I thank my God upon every remembrance of you."

INTRODUCTION

In 1620 a ship left Plymouth, England, carrying the seeds of life as we know it in the United States today. But that voyage, as important as it was, cannot rival the one in AD 52 that embarked from Troas and sailed toward Neapolis.

The apostle Paul, his fellow preacher Silas, Luke the physician and writer, and Paul's disciple Timothy were aboard the vessel that brought the seeds of spiritual life to all of Europe and eventually the United States. Biblical scholars have called this the greatest event in history! For four thousand years, Asia had been the cradle of the human race; now that center was moving to Europe.

As Paul embarked on his second missionary journey, it was his hope to return to all the churches he had visited on his previous excursion. But according to Acts 16:6–7, he was forbidden to go north to Asia or northeast to Bithynia. While in Troas, the Lord spoke to Paul through a vision, in which he saw a man from Macedonia pleading with him to come over and help the people there. Paul's response is recorded by Luke: "Now after he had seen the vision, immediately we sought to go to Macedonia, concluding that the Lord had called us to preach the gospel to them" (16:10).

Paul and his company left Troas via the most direct route to the seaport of Neapolis and from there to the most important city in Macedonia, Philippi. Located about nine miles from the coast of the Aegean Sea, Philippi was a Roman colony and a flourishing, wealthy city. When Paul and his associates arrived there, they found no synagogue; on the Sabbath they assembled at the riverside where worshippers had been gathering regularly for prayer. As a result of that first meeting, Lydia, a merchant woman, was converted and baptized. In gratitude for what the Lord had done in her life, she offered her home as a place of lodging for the missionary team.

As soon as it became evident that the Lord was going to bless His Word, opposition developed. A demon-possessed slave girl began to follow the preachers and associate herself with them by loudly announcing their mission. Within a short time Paul cast the demon out of her, and she too was converted and made whole. The men who owned this girl had been using her for their own gain and were furious. They seized Paul and Silas and had them beaten and thrown in jail. Locked in the inner prison, the two men were placed in stocks, under secure guard. At midnight, as they were singing praises to God, an earthquake broke open the prison and freed all the prisoners from their bonds. The jailer, asleep in the adjoining house, heard the commotion and ran to the prison. Although the night was dark, he could see that the doors were open, and he concluded that the prisoners must have escaped.

Rather than suffer shameful death, he decided to take his own life. He had drawn his sword to kill himself when Paul saw what was about to happen. He told the jailer not to harm himself, because they had not escaped! As a result of this encounter, the jailer and all his family were saved and baptized.

Ten years after the founding of the church in Philippi, while Paul was a prisoner, he wrote to his Macedonian friends. Three times in his letter he expressed his gratitude for the gift they had sent to him by way of Epaphroditus. He had heard they were concerned about him, and he wished to encourage them. But he also had some corrective concerns. He knew that a spirit of division had developed among them, and several times he admonished them to be unified. On six different occasions he referred to the coming day of Christ, reminding them finally that "the Lord is at hand" (Phil. 4:5). He concluded his letter with encouraging words for their anxious hearts.

The theme of this letter is *joy*. The word rejoice is found nine times, the word *joy* four times, and the expression "rejoice with" two times. Even though he was writing as a prisoner, Paul was filled with joy, and that joy permeates his letter. The secret of his joy was his relationship with Jesus Christ. The letter begins and ends with the name of Jesus. Forty times Paul mentioned his beloved Savior's name, eighteen times in chapter 1 alone, which averages at least one citation in every two or three verses.

Paul saw himself as a slave of Christ. He referred to the Philippians as saints in Christ. He described his imprisonment as his bonds in Christ; and even though he knew that some were taking advantage of his imprisonment, he rejoiced that Christ was being preached. He had abandoned all things for the excellency of the knowledge of Jesus Christ, and he spoke of his life as "to live is Christ." For the apostle, even death was defined as being with Christ.

As he admonished the congregation in Philippi to be unified, he expressed his hope that they would "let this mind be in you which was also in Christ Jesus." Even his personal plans were expressed in relationship to his Lord. He trusted in the Lord Jesus to send Timothy to the Philippians, and he trusted in the Lord that he would be able to come to them himself.

He desired to win Christ and to know Christ, and he pointed to heaven from whence also he was looking for the Savior, the Lord Jesus Christ. He concluded his letter by expressing his desire that the "grace of our Lord Jesus Christ" would be with the Philippians.

The reason for Paul's joy was his relationship with Christ! As we study his letter to the Philippians, we will observe the testing of that joy in the crucible of Roman imprisonment. If Paul's relationship to his Master could bring him joy under those conditions, then surely we who also love the Savior can learn to rejoice in our difficult times as well.

David Jeremiah
San Diego, California
1992

Before jumping into your personal or group study, please go to the Readers' Guide at the end of the book.

Paul and Timothy, bondservants of Jesus Christ, to
all the saints in Christ Jesus who are in Philippi,
with the bishops and deacons: Grace to you and peace
from God our Father and the Lord Jesus Christ.

I thank my God upon every remembrance of you,
always in every prayer of mine making request for
you all with joy, for your fellowship in the gospel
from the first day until now, being confident of this
very thing, that He who has begun a good work in
you will complete it until the day of Jesus Christ;
just as it is right for me to think this of you all,
because I have you in my heart, inasmuch as both
in my chains and in the defense and confirmation
of the gospel, you all are partakers with me of
grace. For God is my witness, how greatly I long
for you all with the affection of Jesus Christ.

And this I pray, that your love may abound
still more and more in knowledge and all
discernment, that you may approve the things
that are excellent, that you may be sincere and
without offense till the day of Christ, being filled
with the fruits of righteousness which are by
Jesus Christ, to the glory and praise of God.

Philippians 1:1–11

1

THE JOY OF COMMUNITY
Philippians 1:1–11

Always in every prayer of mine making request for you all with joy.

When Gale Sayers and Brian Piccolo, running backs for the Chicago Bears, began rooming together in the late sixties, it was a first for both of them. Sayers had never had a close relationship with a white person and Piccolo had never really known a black person.

During the 1968 season, Gale Sayers suffered a career-threatening knee injury. Many thought he would never play again. But one year later, after the close of the 1969 season and having made a full recovery, Gale Sayers stood at the banquet of the New York chapter of Professional Football Writers of America to accept the George S. Halas Award as the most courageous player in pro football.

Sayers and Piccolo had planned, with their wives, to sit together at the banquet. Instead, Piccolo was confined to his bed at home. His fight wasn't with a football injury but with cancer.

> That night, Sayers accepted the George S. Halas Award, but he accepted it for Brian Piccolo. As he stood to receive his trophy he said, "You flatter me by giving me this award, but I tell you here and now that I accept it for Brian Piccolo. Brian Piccolo is the man of courage who should receive the George S. Halas Award. It is mine tonight; it is Brian Piccolo's tomorrow. I love Brian Piccolo and I'd like all of you to love him too. Tonight, when you hit your knees, please ask God to love Brian Piccolo."[1]

"I love Brian Piccolo." For some reason, those words sound strange coming from a professional athlete. In our culture, grown men do not usually express their affection so openly.

Before us now is a letter that is filled with expressions of love. As we read this brief letter from Paul to his friends in Philippi, we are immediately struck by the eloquent words he used to describe the deep feelings of attachment he had for all of them.

The small church to which he wrote was located in a Roman colony known as Philippi. For over a decade the members of this church had lived and worked together as a close-knit group of believers. Now, the apostle who had founded the church some ten years earlier could not hide the deep sense of attachment he felt for them. He had been separated from them because of his imprisonment, and he longed for them. His life seemed incomplete without their fellowship. Dr. John Townsend explained in modern terms the pain that was felt by the great apostle:

> The reason is found in the law of entropy, or the second law of thermodynamics. This law of physics states that things that are isolated move toward deterioration.... Entropy operates in the spiritual world, too. Whatever is cut off tends toward deterioration. That's why the ultimate punishment, hell, is not defined by loss of consciousness or annihilation, but by its utter and complete separation from the love of God. Jesus' sacrifice for us involved His own separation from the Father when He became sin on our behalf. He suffered in that "He was cut off out of the land of the living" (Isaiah 53:8). In other words, there is no life without relationship.[2]

Paul's personal relationship with these intimate friends was interrupted because of his imprisonment, but his love for them had not diminished. In fact, his opening remarks in this letter were devoted to a detailed expression of his love for them and the prayer that their love for him and for each other would continue to grow. As Paul communicated his feelings for the Philippians, he touched on many of the key prerequisites for loving relationships within any local assembly. As he concluded his opening remarks, he launched into a prayer for the growth and maturity of these associates for whom he cared so deeply.

HUMILITY: THE ATTITUDE OF LOVE

The letters of the New Testament usually begin with three important details. There is first of all the name of the *sender*, followed by the names of the *subjects*, concluding with the *salutation* or greeting to the readers. The sender of the letter to the Philippians is identified simply as Paul. The name in Latin means "little" or "small." Before God, Paul saw himself as "the least of all the saints" (Eph. 3:8).

As he wrote to his friends in Philippi, Paul was in prison in Rome (Phil. 1:7, 13). When he spoke of his friend Timothy, he referred to them both as fellow "bondservants" of Christ. Later on he spoke of Timothy like this: "As a son with his father he served with me in the gospel" (2:22). In ancient cultures, the sons born to slaves were automatically slaves themselves. Since Timothy was Paul's spiritual son, he inherited his slavehood status.

Paul saw everything in his life through the lens of his slavery to Christ. Outwardly he wrote as a slave of Caesar, but inwardly he considered himself a bondslave to Jesus Christ. He had come to Rome bound in chains, but he referred to these chains as "in Christ" (1:13). To Paul, the term *servant* was a title of dignity and humility. There was no greater position than to be a servant of Jehovah God. We all would do well to remember that God did not save us to become sensations but rather to become servants.

Humble service is a dominant theme in this letter. Besides Paul, Timothy and Epaphroditus are held up as examples of a servant lifestyle. The greatest model of servanthood, however, is Jesus Christ, who took the form of a servant even though He was the sovereign God (2:7). No wonder Paul exhorted believers everywhere to adopt this perspective of life (2:5).

UNITY: THE ATMOSPHERE OF LOVE

While humility is the attitude of love, unity is the atmosphere in which love thrives. The harmony of the Philippian assembly was reflected in this letter first by Paul's reference to the members of the congregation as "all the saints in Christ Jesus who are in Philippi" (1:1). The term *saints* means "set apart ones." Whenever the word *saint* appears in the Bible, it is almost always in the plural form. This is a gentle reminder to us that saints are not meant for isolation but for community. In a letter that Amy Carmichael wrote to her friends in the Dohnavur Fellowship, she painted a graphic picture of our importance to one another in the body of Christ:

> Unlove is deadly. It is a cancer. It may kill slowly, but it always kills in the end. Let us fear it, fear to give room to it as we should fear to nurse a cobra. It is deadlier than any cobra.... One drop of the gall of unlove in my heart or yours, however unseen, has a terrible power of spreading all

through our Family, for we are one body—we are parts of one another. If one member suffers loss, all suffer loss. Not one of us liveth to himself. If unlove be discovered anywhere, stop everything and put it right, if possible, at once.[3]

J. I. Packer also regards fellowship as central to the Christian experience:

We should not ... think of our fellowship with other Christians as a spiritual luxury, an optional addition to the exercises of private devotion. We should recognize rather that such fellowship is a spiritual necessity; for God has made us in such a way that our fellowship with Himself is fed by our fellowship with fellow-Christians, and requires to be so fed constantly for its own deepening and enrichment.[4]

Second, Paul's reference to the bishops and deacons in verse 1 speaks of the unity of this assembly. The bishops were the overseers of the church. The deacons were selected by the church to relieve the pastor of the lesser responsibilities so that his time could be spent in prayer and the study of the word of God (Acts 6:1–7).

There is a mighty sermon on unity contained in that one little word *with*: "the saints ... with the bishops and deacons" (1:1). How blessed is a church where the leaders and the followers stay together! Think about this for just a moment:

> How is leadership to be exercised? What is the relationship between leaders and led? The one word *with* provides the answer.... The strong natural leader chooses the easy path of being out front, taking it for granted that all will follow; the low-profile leader "plays it cool," submerges his own identity and takes the risk that the tail will soon wag the dog. The more demanding exercise, the sterner discipline and the more rewarding way are found in companionate leadership, the saints *with* the overseers and deacons.[5]

If we had designed the structure, the leaders would be the saints and the followers would be the servants. Where there is community, however, the leaders are the servants and the followers are the saints.

Finally, the spirit of unity is exhibited in two greetings. *Grace* is the Gentile greeting, and *peace* is the Jewish greeting. They are spoken together, and in the proper order, for grace must always precede peace. Dr. Alva J. McClain drives home this point:

> You may search the Word of God but you will never find peace first—it is always "grace and peace" never "peace and grace." They are the Siamese twins of the Bible. You cannot have peace until you first have had grace. A man may search and seek until the end of his life, but until

he receives grace through Christ, he can never have peace.[6]

No one illustrates the concept of peace through grace better than John Newton. Although he started out life in a Christian home, he was orphaned at the age of six and ended up living with an agnostic relative. Newton was so abused in this home that he finally ran away and joined the British navy. After serving in the navy for some time, he deserted and ran away to Africa. He openly admitted that he went there for just one purpose: "to sin his fill."

In Africa, he joined forces with a Portuguese slave trader and once again began to experience cruelty. The young Newton ran away to the coast where he was picked up by a slave ship on its way to England. A few days later, John Newton broke into the ship's supply of rum and distributed it to the crew so that they all got drunk. In a stupor, Newton himself fell into the sea and was narrowly saved from drowning by an officer who speared him with a harpoon, leaving a fist-sized scar in his thigh.

Toward the end of the voyage, the ship on which Newton was sailing encountered heavy winds, was blown off course, and began to sink. Newton was sent down into the hold with the slaves and told to man the pumps. He was sure the ship would sink and he would drown. As he worked, he began to cry out to God. He remembered verses he had been taught as a child, and as he remembered them, he was miraculously born again. He went on to become one of England's great teachers of the word of God. Now we can understand the depth of meaning in the words to John Newton's famous hymn:

> Amazing Grace! How sweet the sound
> That saved a wretch like me!
> I once was lost, but now am found;
> Was blind, but now I see.

DIVERSITY: THE ASSIGNMENT OF LOVE

Most people do not find it too difficult to love nice people in an atmosphere of unity. But when their assignment is to love someone who is different, someone with whom they have nothing in common, then love can be a challenge. I am reminded of the well-worn poem that goes like this:

> To love the whole world for me is no chore.
> My only real problem is the guy next door.

The description of the establishment of the church in Philippi (Acts 16) makes it very clear that the membership of the church was very diverse. Along with a Jewish proselyte businesswoman who traded purple cloth from Asia, there was a violent jailer who would have committed suicide if it had not been for Paul. And then there was the slave girl who had been delivered from a demon. They did not have much in common, but they were bound together by God's love. Judson Edwards reminds us that our diversity is a gift from God:

If everybody was just like me ...
The world would sure be a better place to be.
There would be no murder, for I'm not violent.
No stealing, for I'm not a thief.
No adultery, for I'm happily wed.
No atheism, for I believe in God.
No ignorance, for I've been to school.
If only the world was more like me ...
Surely it would be a better place to be.

Or would it?

For if everybody was just like me ...
There would be no merry-go-
rounds, for I get dizzy.
No clowns, for I'm self-conscious.
No doctors, for I hate blood.
No painters, for I'm color blind.
No mechanics, for I can't fix anything.
No elevator operators, for I'm claustrophobic.
No home run kings, for I can't hit a curve.
No balloon riders, for I'm afraid of heights.

> Come to think of it,
> If the world was just like me
> It would be an awfully boring place to be![7]

INTIMACY: THE ACTION OF LOVE

Scholars agree that Philippians is Paul's most personal and intimate letter. In just four chapters, there are over one hundred occurrences of such words as *I*, *me*, and *my*. In fact, the word *I* occurs fifty-two times. As he addressed the people of Philippi in the first few verses, you can feel the depth of his affection. Listen to his words: "I thank my God upon every remembrance of you" (1:3), "I have you in my heart" (1:7), and "I long for you all" (1:8).

It is one thing to love someone; it is quite another to express that love. We were not surprised to learn that Gale Sayers loved Brian Piccolo, but we were taken aback by his expression of that love in a public meeting. If we are honest, we have to admit that unexpressed love is useless to us. The only kind of love we can use is expressed love that we can feel. I say a loud "Amen" to these words of Marian Evans written to a friend in 1875:

> I like not only to be loved, but also to be told
> that I am loved. I am not sure that you are of
> the same kind. But the realm of silence is large
> enough beyond the grave. This is the world of
> literature and speech, and I shall take leave to
> tell you that you are very dear.[8]

One of the greatest evidences of Paul's love for the Philippians was his spirit of gratitude. He was thankful to God each time he remembered them. Seven times in verses 3 through 8, Paul used the pronoun *you* to refer to his close associates in this Macedonian city. I cannot help but wonder if his habit of thanksgiving was the key to his spiritual success. Gratitude pervades all of his letters.

To the Corinthians he wrote, "I thank my God always concerning you" (1 Cor. 1:4).

To the Ephesians, "I ... do not cease to give thanks for you, making mention of you in my prayers" (1:15–16).

To the Colossians it was, "We give thanks to ... God ... praying always for you" (1:3).

To the Thessalonians he wrote, "We give thanks to God always for you all, making mention of you in our prayers" (1 Thess. 1:2).

To Timothy, "I thank God ... as without ceasing I remember you in my prayers" (2 Tim. 1:3).

To Philemon, "I thank my God, making mention of you always in my prayers" (v. 4).

SECURITY: THE AFFIRMATION OF LOVE

As Paul expressed his love for the believers in Philippi, he remembered the long and consistent care they had provided for him. He described that care as "fellowship in the gospel," and he actually had three reference points in mind: "the first day," "now," and "the day of Jesus Christ."

The first day was the day the Lord opened Lydia's heart to the gospel. It was then that she opened her home for the missionaries (Acts 16:14–15). In fact, she opened it so wide that it became the place of assembly for all the early converts at Philippi (16:40). And the Philippian jailer fellowshipped with Paul and Silas in the gospel as he washed their wounds and placed food before them (16:33–34).

That was the first day, and that same spirit continued up to the very day this letter was written. On his second missionary journey, Paul had reached the city of Thessalonica, and the Philippians had once again sent gifts to him to further the work of the gospel: "For even in Thessalonica you sent aid once and again for my necessities" (Phil. 4:16). On that same journey, when Paul came to Corinth and was in need, he did not have to burden the Corinthians because his needs were once again met by "the brethren who came from Macedonia" (2 Cor. 11:9). And when they sent Epaphroditus to check on Paul in prison in Rome, Epaphroditus exhibited the spirit of the church from which he had come. He risked his very life for Paul as a demonstration that the fellowship of "this gospel" had continued from the first day until "now."

Paul knew this good work that God was doing in and through the Philippian believers would continue until still a third day, the day when they would all stand before the Lord to give an account. By their continued support of Paul, these Christians were simply doing what the apostle later described as "working out your own salvation." In other words, what God had *worked in* through the gospel of His Son, Jesus Christ, they were now *working out* through their acts of love (Phil. 2:12–13).

Love that does not act fails to meet the standard set down in God's Word. Paul felt secure in the love of the Philippians, because for almost a decade they had expressed their love in acts of kindness and support. C. S. Lewis reminds us that love by any other definition is misnamed:

> It would be quite wrong to think that the way to become [loving] is to sit trying to manufacture affectionate feelings.... The rule for all of us is perfectly simple. Do not waste time bothering whether you "love" your neighbour; act as if you did. As soon as we do this we find one of the great secrets. When you are behaving as if you loved someone, you will presently come to love him.[9]

Having expressed his love for the Philippians, Paul now prayed that their love for him and for each other would continue to grow to maturity. Listen to the heart of the great apostle as he interceded for his beloved Philippians, that they would grow in four aspects of their spiritual lives.

GROWTH IN SPIRITUAL DEVOTION

"That your love may abound still more and more" (1:9). No matter how much the believers of Philippi loved, Paul prayed that their love would deepen and intensify. He wanted them to go from the *possession* of love to the *progression* of love. That which had characterized this fellowship in the past should continue to overflow until it reached its full potential.

When Paul used the word *abound*, he was talking about the *extent* of their love—love that reached many more people. When he used the phrase "more and more," he was talking about the *effectiveness* of their love. He wanted them to learn how to love more people and love them all better.

The Greek word picture behind the word *abound* is that of a bucket standing under a giant waterfall, with the water flowing over all sides because the bucket cannot possibly contain the downpour. So Paul prayed that the love of the Philippians would continue to grow until it could not be contained.

But true love needs knowledge and discernment to stay in focus. *Knowledge* is a word used some twenty times in the New Testament to convey the idea of knowing about God and spiritual things. *Discernment* moves beyond the acquisition of knowledge to its application. Without *knowledge*, the Philippians would not know *whom* to love. Without *discernment*, they would not know *how* to love. When love is controlled by both of these virtues, it fulfills the highest goals of God and man.

GROWTH IN SPIRITUAL DISCERNMENT

"That you may approve the things that are excellent" (v. 10). Most scholars translate the phrase "approve the things that are excellent" as "test things that differ." It doesn't take much wisdom to select the good instead of the bad, but choosing between the better and the best requires that we know how to test or critique each choice. Our growth in grace is indicated by the discrimination that rules our lives. As we grow, we begin to reject habits and practices we once approved, because we have learned to see beyond the obvious to the significant. In Romans, Paul spoke of this exercise as proving "what is that good and acceptable and perfect will of God" (12:2).

GROWTH IN SPIRITUAL DEVELOPMENT

"That you may be sincere and without offense till the day of Christ" (Phil. 1:10). Sincerity speaks of an absence of hypocrisy. Paul prayed that the believers in Philippi would be genuine in their lives. He wanted them to be real in their walk with the Lord. Just a few verses later, he spoke of some who were preaching Christ "not sincerely" (v. 16). He prayed these believers would develop a genuine and sincere lifestyle. He wanted them to be what they were, all the way through to the core.

Though it is less than eloquent, the best statement I've ever heard about sincerity goes like this:

Be who you is,

because if you is who you ain't,

you ain't who you is.

"Without offense" refers to the ever-present danger of causing a brother to stumble. The Greek word here is *skandalon*. Originally it referred to the part of a trap to which the bait was attached. If a person is an offense, he does that which causes another to fall into one of Satan's traps. Paul's passion was that these believers would live so that no one would ever stumble because of their behavior.

GROWTH IN SPIRITUAL DEPORTMENT

"Being filled with the fruits of righteousness which are by Jesus Christ, to the glory and praise of God" (v. 11). Some of my earliest grade-school report cards had a category called deportment. My parents were usually more concerned about that than the academic marks. That grade told them if I was behaving myself in class. Paul wanted the believers in Philippi to get high marks in deportment. In fact, he prayed that their hearts and lives would produce a rich spiritual harvest. If their roots were in Christ Jesus (1:1), then the harvest should be the fruits of righteousness, which are by Jesus Christ.

If godly love is defined as seeking the best interest of the one loved, then Paul's love for the Philippians certainly qualifies. How blessed they were to be among his disciples!

Author Alan McGinnis shared the story of Viktor Frankl, a Viennese Jew who was interned by the Germans for more than three years. He was moved from one concentration camp to another, even spending several months at Auschwitz. There, he and the other men were awakened each day at 3:00 a.m. for work. McGinnis wrote,

> One morning as they marched out to lay railroad
> ties in the frozen ground miles from camp, the
> accompanying guards kept shouting and driving

them with the butts of their rifles. Anyone with sore feet supported himself on his neighbor's arm. The man next to Frankl, hiding his mouth behind his upturned collar, whispered:

"If our wives could see us now! I do hope they are better off in their camps and don't know what is happening to us."

Frankl writes:

"That brought thoughts of my own wife to mind. And as we stumbled on for miles, slipping on icy spots, supporting each other time and again, dragging one another up and onward, nothing was said, we both knew; each of us was thinking of his wife. Occasionally I looked at the sky, where the stars were fading and the pink light of the morning was beginning to spread behind a dark bank of clouds. But my mind clung to [that picture of my wife] ... imagining it with an uncanny acuteness. I heard her answering me, saw her smile, her frank and encouraging look.

"A thought transfixed me: for the first time in my life I saw the truth as it is set into song by so many poets, proclaimed as the final wisdom by so many thinkers. The truth—that love is the ultimate and the highest goal to which [we] ... can aspire. Then I grasped the meaning of the greatest secret that human poetry and

human thought and belief have to impart: ...
salvation ... is through love and in love."[10]

And Paul would add that there is real joy in loving ... a joy so
genuine, as we shall see in the next chapter, that it can sustain us
even in the midst of adversity.

But I want you to know, brethren, that the things which happened to me have actually turned out for the furtherance of the gospel, so that it has become evident to the whole palace guard, and to all the rest, that my chains are in Christ; and most of the brethren in the Lord, having become confident by my chains, are much more bold to speak the word without fear.

Some indeed preach Christ even from envy and strife, and some also from goodwill: The former preach Christ from selfish ambition, not sincerely, supposing to add affliction to my chains; but the latter out of love, knowing that I am appointed for the defense of the gospel. What then? Only that in every way, whether in pretense or in truth, Christ is preached; and in this I rejoice, yes, and will rejoice.

For I know that this will turn out for my deliverance through your prayer and the supply of the Spirit of Jesus Christ, according to my earnest expectation and hope that in nothing I shall be ashamed, but with all boldness, as always, so now also Christ will be magnified in my body, whether by life or by death. For to me, to live is Christ, and to die is gain. But if I live on in the flesh, this will mean fruit from my labor; yet what I shall choose I cannot tell. For I am hard-pressed between the two, having a desire to depart and be with Christ, which is far better. Nevertheless to remain in the flesh is more needful for you. And being confident of this, I know that I shall remain and continue with you all for your progress and joy of faith, that your rejoicing for me may be more abundant in Jesus Christ by my coming to you again.

Philippians 1:12–26

THE JOY OF ADVERSITY

Philippians 1:12–26

Whether in pretense or in truth, Christ is preached;
and in this I rejoice, yes, and will rejoice.

It was the bottom of the sixth inning. The Montreal Expos' most feared hitter, Tim Raines, was at the plate. The pitcher glared at the catcher and checked the runner on first base. Then, kicking high, he pushed off the rubber and threw as hard as he could. It was the last pitch he would ever throw. A loud, sickening crack was heard all over the stadium. Weakened by undiscovered cancer, the humerus bone in Dave Dravecky's pitching arm had snapped in two. "My arm felt like I'd been hit with a meat axe," said the San Francisco Giants' and former San Diego Padres' hurler. He grabbed his arm to keep it from flying toward home plate as he screamed, tumbling headfirst to the ground.[1]

While his baseball career was over, his adversity had just begun. After many examinations, the doctors told him that his pitching arm would have to be amputated at the shoulder to guarantee that the cancer would not spread to other parts of his body.

I can't imagine what Dave must have felt as the reality of that news set in. He was in the prime of his career, and under normal circumstances could have expected to play baseball for many more years. But now it was over.

Several weeks after his surgery, Dave Dravecky came back to Jack Murphy Stadium to say thanks to his many San Diego friends. He was greeted with a standing ovation. As on every other speaking assignment since he came out of the recovery room minus his left arm, he glorified God and gave praise to the name of Jesus.[2]

The day after his appearance at the stadium, I read in the *San Diego Union* that he had received over seven hundred invitations to speak during the next year. The apparent tragedy in his life had begun to take on a look of victory!

God often has hidden purposes in the adversity He allows. I am reminded that several letters in the New Testament are called Prison Epistles. Paul wrote these letters, including the letter to the Philippians, while he was incarcerated. The book of Revelation was penned by the apostle John while he was in exile on the island of Patmos. It was in prison that John Bunyan saw the great vision that later became the immortal *Pilgrim's Progress*. The prisons of our lives can often become places of great opportunity and ministry. Charles Colson, the famed Watergate conspirator, concluded his book *Loving God* with this analogy:

> My lowest days as a Christian (and there were low
> ones—seven months' worth of them in prison, to
> be exact) have been more fulfilling and rewarding
> than all the days of glory in the White House.[3]

And it was that way for the apostle Paul. When he referred in verse 12 to "the things which happened to me," he was reminding the Philippians that he had experienced some difficult days. He was writing to them in response to a letter from the Philippian church that had been carried to him by Epaphroditus. These believers in Philippi loved Paul dearly and were very concerned about his welfare. For two years he had been a prisoner in Caesarea and now he was a prisoner in Rome. Because Paul knew of their concern, he set out to put their minds at ease.

What were the things that happened to Paul? Although he did not itemize them in his letter, Luke told the story in Acts 20–28, and Paul himself summarized his troubles in 2 Corinthians 11:23–27.

By his own testimony, we know Paul had a great desire to preach the gospel in Rome.

- Acts 19:21—"After I have been there [Jerusalem], I must also see Rome."
- Romans 1:15—"So, as much as is in me, I am ready [eager] to preach the gospel to you who are in Rome also."

- Acts 23:11—"The following night the Lord stood by him and said, 'Be of good cheer, Paul; for as you have testified for Me in Jerusalem, so you must also bear witness at Rome.'"

When Paul prayed that he might have a prosperous journey to Rome in the will of God (Rom. 1:10), I'm sure he had no idea how that prayer would be answered. As Warren Wiersbe has observed, he wanted to go as a *preacher* but ended up going as a *prisoner.*[4]

Paul's difficulties actually began when he arrived in Jerusalem. It was there he was warned that afflictions and imprisonment awaited him (Acts 20:22–23).

In spite of the testimony of his dynamic conversion, he was falsely accused, nearly lynched by a religious mob, and finally ended up in a Roman prison. He would have been beaten but for the fact that he pleaded his Roman citizenship. Everything about his imprisonment was a mockery. He was insulted and shamed.

And then there was the journey to Rome—the storm at sea … his life hanging in the balance. When finally he did arrive in Rome, it was not as he had hoped. He came with the condemned in chains and waited two full years before he knew the outcome of his appeal.

And yet Paul was still certain that this sorrow and suffering was part of God's plan for his life. When writing to the Corinthians, he said, "Therefore I take pleasure in infirmities, in reproaches, in needs, in persecutions, in distresses, for Christ's sake. For when I am weak, then I am strong" (2 Cor. 12:10).

The words *take pleasure* mean "to think well" or "to have the right attitude." As he relayed his situation to his friends in Philippi, Paul clearly had the right attitude toward his troubles. His upbeat explanation has become a source of great encouragement to all who have walked through the valley. Here, then, from Paul's letter are seven proven principles that will encourage us when we face trouble.

ADVERSITY PROMOTES THE PROGRESS OF THE GOSPEL

When Paul talked about his present situation, he did not discuss his personal discomfort. He was not occupied with the inconvenience that imprisonment had caused him. His concern was for the gospel and its advance. He told his prayer supporters in Philippi that his imprisonment had actually put the gospel ahead of schedule in Rome.

When he described the advance of the gospel, he used the word *furtherance*. This is a military term used by engineers who would prepare a road for an advancing army by removing obstructions such as rocks and trees. Paul viewed his imprisonment as the removal of barriers to the gospel in Rome. One writer expressed it this way:

> [As Paul looks back over these events] he stresses … the masses of dark threads that the

recent years had woven into the pattern of his life—the animosities and bodily pains, the lies, misrepresentations and deceitfulness, the miscarriage of justice, the chains, ... the mental turmoil of appealing to Caesar against his own people, the nearness of death and the diminution of hope, the triumph of wickedness and the continued suppression of the truth. He invites us to take these things and look them in the face, for it is these which have resulted—contrary to what their surface appearance might have suggested—in the progress of the gospel.[5]

Just as Dave Dravecky would never have received seven hundred invitations to speak about Christ's work in his life without his encounter with cancer, so Paul recognized that without his imprisonment, the influence of the gospel in Rome would have been retarded.

ADVERSITY PROVIDES OPPORTUNITIES FOR WITNESS

When the apostle spoke of his bonds being manifested in all the palace, he was referring to the Praetorian Guard, which was a chosen division of crack imperial troops. They were paid well and given special assignments, one of which was to guard the prisoners who were waiting for an audience with Caesar.

These guards would have been exposed to Paul's testimony as he shared it with them personally and as they listened to him share it with others.

Apart from his imprisonment, there would have been no way Paul could have approached the highest dignitaries in the palace in Rome. We know that some of them became Christians because of the final words of Paul in this very letter. He referred to "the saints … who are of Caesar's household" (4:22).

For twenty-four hours a day he was chained to a Roman soldier. Every six hours the shift changed, so Paul had four prospects for salvation every day of the week. During his two-year imprisonment, he would have been able to engage in almost three thousand witnessing opportunities with Rome's top military personnel.

If you compare Philippians 1:13 with Acts 28:30–31, you see that Paul had great freedom even though he was a prisoner: "Then Paul dwelt two whole years in his own rented house, and received all who came to him, preaching the kingdom of God and teaching the things which concern the Lord Jesus Christ with all confidence, no one forbidding him."

When he added to his mention of the Praetorian Guard the phrase "to all the rest," he revealed the fact that his imprisonment was making an impact on everyone in the palace. He had the opportunity to witness to other soldiers, household servants, and government officials.

In her first book, Corrie ten Boom told of her experience in Ravensbrück prison during World War II. As she reflected on her own pain and suffering, she came to understand that one of God's purposes was that her suffering should benefit others:

> God had brought me here for a specific task. I was here to lead the sorrowing and the despairing to the Savior. I was to see how He comforted them. I was to point the way to heaven to people among whom were many that would soon be dying.[6]

Marine Lieutenant Clebe McClary was permanently disabled when an enemy grenade exploded in his foxhole. His evaluation of his adversity is similar to that of Corrie ten Boom:

> I don't think my suffering was in vain. The Lord has used my experiences for good by drawing many lives to Him. It's hard to see any good that came from the war in Vietnam, but I don't believe our effort was wasted. Surely some seed was planted for Christ that cannot be stamped out.[7]

Like the many others who have suffered after him, Paul allowed his adversity to become a platform for the gospel. What the Enemy hoped would thwart the gospel actually advanced it. If for no other reason than this, we should think twice before we complain about our difficult situations. It just might be that God is up to something eternal!

ADVERSITY PRODUCES COURAGE IN OUR FELLOW BELIEVERS

It is evident that Paul's imprisonment had an effect on his associates. He was aware that many of them became very confident and bold because they saw his courage. Bravery is contagious! Persecution can be productive! One has to wonder what would have become of the gospel had it not been for persecution. It was often the impetus to evangelism: "At that time a great persecution arose against the church which was at Jerusalem; and they were all scattered.... Therefore those who were scattered went everywhere preaching the word" (Acts 8:1, 4).

In seventeenth-century England, George Fox and the Quakers were making their mark for the gospel and hundreds were being converted. In the midst of the revival, while preaching at the Castle of Carlisle in the north of England, George Fox was arrested on charges of blasphemy. After his trial he was thrown into a filthy dungeon overrun with vermin and criminals. No one was allowed even a glimpse of him. Some who tried to bring him food were clubbed back by the jailers. But 150 miles away, sixteen-year-old James Parnell, a cripple endowed with a brilliant mind, heard about Fox's situation and walked the long miles to the prison. Somehow he managed to get in, and he was never the same again. Says Walter Williams, in his volume on Quaker history, "After he and George Fox spent some time in fellowship together, the lad left Carlisle dungeon with heart aflame, and gave the rest of his life to Christ and the Friends Movement."[8]

In my lifetime I have witnessed the infectious impact of courageous suffering. The deaths of Paul Carlson, missionary to the Congo; Jim Elliot, missionary to Ecuador's Auca Indians; and Chet Bitterman, missionary to Colombia, have probably been responsible for more missionary recruits than any other recent motivating force.

ADVERSITY PROVES THE CHARACTER OF OUR FRIENDSHIPS

As Paul looked out upon the church, he saw encouraging things, but he also saw many discouraging things. He saw not only those who were supporting him in his trials but also those who were taking advantage of his trials and attempting to afflict him. These were not false teachers, because Paul said they preached Christ. He rejoiced in the *message* they preached, but he was grieved by the *manner* in which they delivered it. They preached from envy and partisanship. Paul chose not to dwell on what they did to him; we don't know exactly what it was, but we do know that their private lives were not consistent with their public lives.

As Paul described those who were preaching for the wrong reasons, he used an interesting word. He said they were preaching out of *contention*. That word means "to canvass for office in order to get people to support you." Their aim was to get people to follow them. Paul's aim was to get people to follow Christ.

As he sorted this out, he tried to come to some resolution in the matter. He rejoiced that Christ was being preached, even if it was not as he wanted it to be. He knew that though Christ might not honor the motive of the messenger, He would honor and bless His Word.

ADVERSITY PROVOKES GROWTH IN OUR LIVES

Two men are shot down in Vietnam and imprisoned in the infamous Hoa Lo prison. They are isolated, chained to cement slabs, and continuously beaten with rusty shackles and tortured for information. Yet although these men are receiving the same abuse, they form radically different beliefs about their experience. One man decides that his life is over, and in order to avoid any additional pain, commits suicide. The other pulls from these brutalizing events a deeper belief in himself, his fellow man, and his Creator than he's ever had before. Today Captain Gerald Coffee uses his experience of this to remind people all over the world of the power of the human spirit to overcome virtually any level of pain, any challenge, or any problem.[9]

Adversity separates men! It makes some better; it makes others bitter. Over eighty years ago, a well-known psychologist wrote:

Most people live, whether physically, intellectually or morally, in a very restricted circle of their potential being. They make use of a very small portion of their possible consciousness, of their soul's resources in general, much like a man who, out of his whole bodily organism, should get into a habit of using and moving only his little finger. *Great emergencies and crises show us how much greater our vital resources are than we had supposed.*[10]

As Paul faced the adversity of his circumstances, he saw the advantages. When he spoke of these events resulting in his salvation, he was not talking about his conversion to Christ but about his continued growth in Christ. In 1:6 he plainly stated his conviction that God, who had begun that good work on the first day, would continue to perform it until the day of Jesus Christ. As he looked at his confinement, he saw it as another method of bringing him to his ultimate goal of Christian maturity. There were three things at work in his life accomplishing this goal.

First of all, there were the *prayers of his friends.* Paul knew the Philippians were praying for him. Earlier in this letter, Paul said, "I pray" (1:9). Now he was depending on the fact that they were praying also. In fact, in almost all his letters, Paul cited the mutuality of prayer. What he himself practiced, he also profited from, as it was lived out in others.

In Romans he said, "I make mention of you always in my prayers…. Now I beg you, brethren, through the Lord Jesus

Christ, and through the love of the Spirit, that you strive together with me in prayers to God for me" (1:9; 15:30).

In Ephesians he said, "[I] do not cease to give thanks for you, making mention of you in my prayers.... Finally, my brethren ... praying always ... for me" (1:16; 6:10, 18–19).

In 1 Thessalonians he wrote, "Making mention of you in our prayers ... night and day.... Brethren, pray for us" (1:2; 3:10; 5:25).

In 2 Thessalonians he wrote, "Therefore we also pray always for you.... Finally, brethren, pray for us" (1:11; 3:1).

Often, when facing trouble, we are the focus of the prayers of God's people. It is through these prayers that we are able to survive our crises and go on to maturity. As members of God's earthly family, we should not forget to put the spiritual growth of others at the top of our prayer lists. When we are experiencing growing pains, it is good to know that someone is praying. I have always loved the stark contrast of the two phrases of this verse: "Peter was therefore kept in prison, but constant prayer was offered to God for him by the church" (Acts 12:5).

Second, Paul was not only sustained by the prayers of his friends but was also encouraged by the *provision of the Holy Spirit*. His language is picturesque; this phrase literally means, "the full supply of the Holy Spirit."

If you have ever known the Holy Spirit drawing close to you in moments of crisis, then you understand why He is called the Comforter.

David Jacobsen was a hostage in Beirut for seventeen months. He was head of the largest hospital in West Beirut when, one day in 1985, three hooded men wielding machine guns took him captive. He was taken, bound and gagged, from one hideout to another and spent most of his time on a cold dirt floor, chained to the wall. Once a day he was fed an unpalatable mush of water, rice, and lentils.

As an American, Jacobsen was hated by his captors. He was just a political pawn and was treated cruelly. Instead of breaking his spirit, however, this made him stronger. He wrote:

> I discovered that no one's faith was weakened by
> the hell we found ourselves in…. We hostages …
> founded the Church of the Locked Door, a name
> we chose with some ruefulness. Grasping hands,
> we'd quote Scripture and pray. Oddly, our guards
> seemed to respect this ritual. Our togetherness in
> prayer showed me that when the Holy Comforter
> is called, He answers.[11]

Jacobsen was released in November 1986, but in his final forty-five days of captivity, he was alone in a six-by-six cell, his muscles and joints cramped by confinement and the damp, aching cold. Yet he said, "The presence of God, the Great Comforter, was stronger than ever."[12]

Paul's own *personal determination* was the third dynamic at work during this time of confinement. He was confident that he would come through this ordeal and see his friends in Philippi again. To describe his attitude, he used the term "earnest expectation." This Greek word has three elements wrapped up in its meaning. It is made up of the words *away, the head*, and *to watch*. Together, they convey the idea of watching something so intently that your head is turned away from everything else. Paul had a single focus in his life. His earnest expectation and hope were mixed with great determination.

- He was determined to keep a clear conscience. "That in nothing I shall be ashamed." Even though under pressure in a Roman prison, Paul was determined to live a holy and righteous life. He would not use his adversity as an excuse for a spiritual relapse.
- He was determined to keep a courageous testimony. "With all boldness, as always, so now." Paul was also determined to use his adversity as an opportunity to more loudly proclaim Christ. While many are silenced by adversity, Paul actually turned the volume up louder.
- He was determined to keep a Christ-centered focus. "Christ will be magnified in my body, whether by life or by death." From the human viewpoint, Paul's body was fairly useless to him, since he was chained to a soldier twenty-four hours each day. But Paul saw beyond all that.

He was determined that his body would be a vehicle for magnifying Christ. In one of his letters to Timothy, he described his situation like this: "I suffer trouble as an evildoer, even to the point of chains; but the word of God is not chained" (2 Tim. 2:9). Guy King suggests some of the ways the body can magnify the Lord:

> Christ magnified in the body—magnified by lips that bear happy testimony to Him; magnified by hands employed in His service; magnified by feet only too happy to go on His errands; magnified by shoulders happy to bear one another's burdens.[13]

When we magnify Christ, we do not do it *microscopically*. A microscope takes that which is little and makes it big. Our Lord is not little! Then we must magnify Him *telescopically*. We must take the Lord, who is far away from so many, and bring Him close at hand. Quite often the Lord uses the adversity in our lives as a lens through which He can be seen! In the process of it all, He is developing our character so that we can be worthy reflectors of His glory. Paul teaches us that character cannot be developed in ease and quiet. Only through experiences of trials and suffering can the soul be strengthened.

Adoniram Judson, famous missionary to Burma, is an illustration of this attitude. After fourteen years on the mission field, what did he have to show for his labors? The graves of his wife and all his children, imprisonments and diseases so awful that once he wrote, "If I had not felt certain that every additional trial was ordered by infinite love and mercy, I could not have survived my accumulated sufferings!" But he never thought of quitting. At the very lowest ebb of his career, he prayed that "he might live to translate the entire Bible into the native language, and to preside over a native church of at least one hundred members."[14]

Helen Keller suffered an illness at eighteen months that left her completely blind and deaf. For five years she was isolated from the world and alone in darkness. Then with the help of Anne Sullivan, Helen fought back against her handicap. She never pitied herself; she never gave up. She once said:

> The marvelous richness of human experience would lose something of rewarding joy if there were no limitations to overcome. The hilltop hour would not be half so wonderful if there were not dark valleys to traverse.[15]

ADVERSITY PURIFIES OUR MOTIVES

In what most scholars think is the key verse of this entire letter, Paul stated his life's motive and mission clearly. For him, to live was Christ and to die was gain. No wonder his life had such power and momentum. He forced every experience of life through the grid of his personal purpose statement. He knew what he was all about. The suffering of his present situation was not intolerable, because he saw it as a part of God's plan and his own stated purpose.

When we know who we are, why we are here, and where we are going, we can confidently face each day, and even difficulties take on new meaning. Then, as Alec Motyer illustrates, everything becomes something for Jesus:

> Two friends were talking together, one older and wise, the other younger and passing through a severe testing-time. The older friend, with loving wisdom, said, "No moment will ever again be like this; let there be something for Jesus in it." It is not "something for Jesus" if we dwell on our miseries; nor if we let opportunities pass without a word about our Lord; nor if we think that any hand other than his brought us to that place. It is "something for Jesus" if we think and speak about him and his glory; it is "something for him" if we acknowledge and trust his all-sovereign will.[16]

ADVERSITY PREPARES US TO SEE LIFE AND DEATH IN PERSPECTIVE

When a Christian faces adversity, especially if it is intense and prolonged, his perspective on life and death is brought into sharp focus. For Paul, the issue was not his desire to die in order to escape suffering. Paul loved life and accepted his imprisonment as part of God's perfect plan for him. He also knew what God had planned for his future. As he contemplated his present joy and compared it to the promised joy of heaven, he found himself caught between two loves. H. C. G. Moule adequately summarizes his dilemma: "Life and death look to us like two evils of which we know not which is the less. As for the apostle, they look to him like two immense blessings, of which he knows not which is the better."[17]

In other words, Paul saw life and death as equally desirable. If he continued to live, he would come to know and love and serve the Lord more fully. If he died, he would completely and finally and perfectly know Him. He was caught between his *desire* to be with Christ personally and his sense of *duty* to help the Philippians. Paul's selfless servant heart is unmatched, outside of Christ Jesus. William Hendriksen's chart visualizes the dilemma the apostle faced as he compared the advantages of life and death:

Remaining Here	Departing to Be with Christ
A temporary residence	Permanent abode
Suffering mixed with joy	Joy unmixed with suffering
Suffering for a while	Joy forever
Being absent from the Lord	Being at home with the Lord
The fight	The feast
The realm of sin	The realm of complete deliverance from sin; positive holiness[18]

Looking back over the apostle's statement about trouble, we discover there are indeed advantages to adversity:

1. Adversity promotes the progress of the gospel.
2. Adversity provides opportunities to witness.
3. Adversity produces courage in our fellow believers.
4. Adversity proves the character of our friendships.
5. Adversity provokes growth in our lives.
6. Adversity purifies our motives.
7. Adversity prepares us to see life and death in perspective.

A woman whose heart was crushed by a tragedy, which happened through no fault of her own, wrote her pastor, "Your advice to stop asking *why* helped a lot. And your sermon yesterday helped to make us able to say, 'We will,' and leave it in God's hands. We will let Him use even this, till His plan is perfected." And then she added this bit of verse, which better than anything I have seen summarizes the message of this section of Paul's letter to the Philippians:

The things that happen unto me
Are not by chance, I know,
But because my Father's wisdom
Has willed to have it so.
For the "furtherance of the gospel"

As a part of His great plan,
God can use our disappointments
And the weaknesses of man.

Give me faith to meet them bravely,
Trials I do not understand,
To let God work His will in me—
To trust His guiding hand.
Help me to shine, a clear bright light,
And not to live in vain—
Help me hold forth the Word of life
In triumph over pain.[19]

Only let your conduct be worthy of the gospel of Christ, so that whether I come and see you or am absent, I may hear of your affairs, that you stand fast in one spirit, with one mind striving together for the faith of the gospel, and not in any way terrified by your adversaries, which is to them a proof of perdition, but to you of salvation, and that from God. For to you it has been granted on behalf of Christ, not only to believe in Him, but also to suffer for His sake, having the same conflict which you saw in me and now hear is in me.

Philippians 1:27–30

3

THE JOY OF INTEGRITY

Philippians 1:27–30

*Stand fast in one spirit, with one mind striving
together for the faith of the gospel.*

During the Vietnam War, a GI helicopter pilot was killed. On his tombstone in New Hampshire his parents inscribed these words by John Stuart Mill:

> War is an ugly thing, but not the ugliest of things. The decayed and degraded state of moral and patriotic feeling, which thinks nothing is worth a war, is worse. A man who has nothing which he cares more about than his own personal safety is a miserable creature, and has no chance of being free unless he is made free and kept so by the exertions of better men than himself.[1]

In his book *Against the Night*, Charles Colson laments the fact that our culture has deteriorated to such an extent that individualism reigns supreme. No one cares about anyone else, and no one is willing to stand up for the moral convictions that hold society together. To illustrate his point, Colson remembered this incident:

> In 1978, during President Carter's attempt to reinstate draft registration, newspapers across the country carried a photo that I have carried in my mind ever since: a young Princeton student defiantly wielding a poster emblazoned with the words, "Nothing is worth dying for."[2]

Someone said that a man who refuses to stand for something will sooner or later fall for anything. Because of his stand for the faith, Paul was facing the possibility of death, and he was willing to pay the supreme price if called upon to do so. In writing to the Philippian believers, he shared his concern about their willingness to stand against the pressure of persecution. He hoped that he might be with them in person to encourage them if such occurred, but he had no guarantee. So he sent them a strategy that would serve them well, even if he was not available to personally cheer them on.

Paul's game plan for the Philippians is needed in our day too. We are in the minority, surrounded by the Enemy, and constantly being undermined by members of our own army. Many among God's people have adopted a philosophy that gives to survival the attributes of victory. But in our day, as in Paul's, anything short of victory is just the postponement of defeat!

Like a coach presenting his game plan to the players, Paul sent to his friends in Philippi his four priorities for success.

PRIORITY ONE: CONDUCT

While it was never intended in the original language, Paul's first word of instruction is a play on words. When he said, "Let your *conduct* be worthy of the gospel," he used a Greek word, *politeuo*, which means "citizenship." *Politeuo* is derived from the noun *polis*, which means "city." We have carried this word over into the names of some of our American cities, such as Indianapolis and Minneapolis. When we speak of a metropolis or a metropolitan area, we are talking about a city. We also get our words *politics* and *police* from this same root word.

In the Greek age, the *polis* was the largest political unit, and the citizens belonged to the *polis*, or city, in exactly the same way that we belong to our country. So the word as it is used in this verse refers to the public duties of good citizens.

The Philippians would have better understood Paul's comments than we do today. Their city had become a Roman colony through a series of events that included a civil war between Octavian and Anthony. After the war, a number of soldiers who had been favorable toward Anthony settled in Philippi; for that reason, it was declared a Roman colony, a miniature Rome. As such, it was given special privileges; although it was eight hundred miles from Rome, Philippi was Italian soil and the citizens of the city had their names on the rolls in Rome and considered themselves Romans.

The Philippians were very proud of their Roman citizenship. They believed they were Rome's representatives to a culture that was predominantly Greek. So when Paul wrote to the Philippians that he wished them to conduct themselves as good citizens, he was using an aspect of their culture to encourage them to be good citizens of another kingdom to which they also now belonged.

He came right out and said it in Philippians 3:20: "For our citizenship is in heaven, from which we also eagerly wait for the Savior, the Lord Jesus Christ." James Moffatt translated it, "We are a colony of heaven." These believers were "fellow citizens with the saints and members of the household of God" (Eph. 2:19).

Now, as he wrote to them about their heavenly citizenship, he exhorted them to allow their allegiance to control their conduct. Just as they were to live by the laws of their native land, so they were now expected to live by heaven's laws and extend heaven's influence into their pagan culture. A church leader in the second century described the way early Christians followed these instructions:

> While they dwell in Greek or barbarian cities according as each man's lot has been cast, and follow the customs of the land in clothing and food, and other matters of daily life, yet the condition of citizenship which they exhibit is wonderful and admittedly strange. They live in countries of

their own, but simply as sojourners ... enduring the lot of foreigners.... They exist in the flesh, but they live not after the flesh. They spend their existence upon earth, but their citizenship is in heaven. They obey the established laws, and in their own lives they surpass the laws. They love all men, and are persecuted by all.[3]

This encouragement to live worthily of the gospel is the third mention of the gospel in Philippians 1. In verse 7 there is the defense of the gospel; in verses 12–18 there is the proclamation of the gospel; and here in verse 27 there is the testimony of the gospel. All three are important!

As Caesar Augustus may have instructed his soldiers to make sure their conduct was worthy of Roman citizenship, even though they were surrounded by Greeks, so Paul instructed the Philippian Christians to remember that their citizenship was in heaven and they were to conduct themselves in a manner worthy of the gospel. If they were to win the war against the Enemy, they would have to make their conduct priority number one.

Some words written by the apostle Peter help to explain the logic behind this priority:

Your conduct among the surrounding peoples in your different countries should always be good and right, so that although they may in the usual way slander you as evil-doers yet when disasters come, they may glorify God when they see how well you conduct yourselves. (1 Pet. 2:12 PHILLIPS)

PRIORITY TWO: CONSISTENCY

Paul was quite confident he would be acquitted at his trial and set free. He felt sure he would see the Philippians again, but he wanted them to know that his presence or absence should not affect the way they lived their faith.

It is one thing to live the Christian life when our support system is intact. When the people who have discipled us are standing by, we feel secure. But unlike many leaders of our day, Paul desired for his converts a spirit of independence. He knew he would not always be available to help them.

One of the great illustrations of a consistent lifestyle is the Old Testament character Daniel, who proved it is possible to maintain one's integrity even when totally isolated. As a young man, he was carried away captive to the city of Babylon. For seventy years he endured the pressures of a pagan culture. In the first chapter of the book that bears his name, we are given a simple description of his integrity: "Daniel continued until the first year of King Cyrus" (1:21).

Throughout all the captivity, during all the troubles of his nation, through intrigues, envies, murders, and persecutions, Daniel continued. The rule of the kingdom passed from Nebuchadnezzar to Belshazzer to Darius and finally to Cyrus, but Daniel just continued. He was in the public eye all his life; he was in the court from his youth up; he spent the majority of his years in a wicked culture; and *he continued*. So consistent was his life that when the jealous presidents and princes tried to find something against him, "they could find no charge or fault, because he was faithful; nor was there any error or fault found in him" (6:4).

My friend Warren Wiersbe believes a lack of integrity is the major crisis facing the evangelical church of today:

> For nineteen centuries, the church has been telling the world to admit its sins, repent, and believe the Gospel. Today, in the twilight of the twentieth century, the world is telling the church to face up to her sins, repent, and start being the true church of that Gospel. We Christians boast that we are not ashamed of the Gospel of Christ, but perhaps the Gospel of Christ is ashamed of us. For some reason, our ministry doesn't match our message.[4]

In his book *A Severe Mercy*, Sheldon Vanauken expressed a similar thought:

> The best argument for Christianity is Christians: their joy, their certainty, their completeness. But the strongest argument *against* Christianity is also Christians—when they are somber and joyless, when they are self-righteous and smug ... then Christianity dies a thousand deaths.[5]

PRIORITY THREE: COOPERATION

Most of all, Paul wished the Philippians to understand that they would not be able to survive the pressures alone. They must stand fast in the Lord, but they would need to do so while joining hands with each other. Paul sounded the challenge to stand fast in many of his other letters as well.

To the Corinthians he wrote, "Watch, stand fast in the faith, be brave, be strong" (1 Cor. 16:13).

To the Galatians he wrote, "Stand fast therefore in the liberty by which Christ has made us free, and do not be entangled again with a yoke of bondage" (5:1).

To the Thessalonians he wrote, "Therefore, brethren, stand fast and hold the traditions which you were taught, whether by word or our epistle" (2 Thess. 2:15).

Winston Churchill once wrote about General Tudor, the British commander of a division facing the Germans in an assault in March 1918: "The impression I had of Tudor was of an iron peg, hammered into the frozen ground, immovable."[6] In the war the odds were heavily against him, but Tudor knew how to meet an apparently irresistible force. He merely stood firm and let the force expend itself on him. That is how Paul wanted his friends in Philippi to respond to the pressures around them.

While the apostle was concerned about the attitude of the believers toward those who were outside the fellowship, he was also concerned about the love of the believers for those inside the fellowship. He shared that concern again later on in this letter (Phil. 2:2–3; 4:1). It is also conveyed in many of the letters that he wrote to the other churches (Rom. 12:5–12; 1 Cor. 1:10; 10:17; 2 Cor. 13:11; Gal. 3:28; Eph. 2:11–22; 4:3–4, 13).

When he instructed them to "strive together," he used the word from which we get our word *athlete*. This is a special unity of striving together or struggling side by side, like athletes against a common opponent. English poet and novelist Rudyard Kipling penned a verse that visualizes this:

> Now this is the law of the jungle
> As old and as true as the sky;
> And the wolf that keep it may prosper,
> And the wolf that shall break it must die.
> As the creeper that girdles the tree trunk,
> The law runneth forward and back—
> And the strength of the pack is the wolf
> And the strength of the wolf is the pack.[7]

When it comes to standing for truth in times of pressure, the law of the jungle is in force. The strength of the church is the Christian, and the strength of the Christian is the church.

PRIORITY FOUR: COURAGE

Paul knew from experience that there would be many occasions for the Philippians to demonstrate courage beyond what they personally possessed. He provided guidelines to help them accurately identify those times and to draw strength from each other and from Christ.

COURAGE TO ENCOUNTER PERSECUTION

Paul warned the Philippians not to be terrified by their enemies. The word *terrified* was used of horses that were frightened or spooked into an uncontrollable stampede. It is inward fear caused by an outward stimulus. This is the only place in the New Testament where this particular word is used, and it is very appropriate for the little group of believers living in Philippi during a violent period of history.

We are not told who the adversaries were, but they could easily have been the ones Paul described later as "dogs,… evil workers,… the enemies of the cross of Christ: whose end is destruction, whose god is their belly, and whose glory is in their shame—who set their mind on earthly things" (3:2, 18–19).

This courage in the face of opposition is a double-edged sword. It is evidence of the believers' salvation and of their enemies' doom. The inability of their enemies to intimidate them becomes proof of the genuineness of their faith.

Most scholars date Paul's writing of the letter to the Philippians around AD 60–63. If this is accurate, then the pressure in the Roman Empire was growing. For it was in July AD 64 that Emperor Nero surpassed himself in cruelty when he ordered his servants to set fire to Rome. Tacitus, one of the few eyewitness historians of that day, told about it:

> Consequently, to get rid of the report [that he
> had ordered the fire], Nero fastened the guilt and
> inflicted the most exquisite tortures on a class

hated for their abominations, called Christians by the populace. Christus, from whom the name had its origin, suffered the extreme penalty during the reign of Tiberius at the hands of one of our procurators, Pontius Pilatus, and a most mischevious superstition, thus checked for the moment, again broke out not only in Judæa, the first source of the evil, but even in Rome, where all things hideous and shameful from every part of the world find their centre and become popular. Accordingly, an arrest was first made of all who pleaded guilty; then, upon their information, an immense multitude was convicted, not so much of the crime of firing the city, as of hatred against mankind. Mockery of every sort was added to their deaths. Covered with the skins of beasts, they were torn by dogs and perished, or were nailed to crosses, or were doomed to the flames.[8]

No doubt some of those who read this letter from Paul would experience this suffering. Then they would remember Paul's words and remember that he too had suffered as a prisoner and had maintained the integrity of his faith.

COURAGE TO ENDURE PAIN

Paul regarded suffering for Christ as a privilege. In fact, twice in these last verses of chapter 1, he referred to persecution as a gift from God. In verse 28 we are told that to suffer is "from God." In verse 29 we read that "it has been granted on behalf of Christ … to suffer for His sake." Please note that the blessing is in suffering for Him. No one goes around looking for suffering, but suffering on behalf of Christ and His gospel is different. Jesus said such suffering is a blessing (Matt. 5:11–12).

John Huss (1369–1415) was the rector of Charles University in Prague when he was thrown into prison for advocating the doctrines of the Reformation. Two weeks before he was martyred for his faith, Huss wrote these words from his prison cell:

> I am greatly consoled by that saying of Christ, "Blessed are ye when men shall hate you." … It bids us rejoice in these tribulations.… It is easy to read it aloud and expound it, but difficult to live out.…
>
> O Most Holy Christ … give me a fearless heart, a right faith, a firm hope, a perfect love, that for Thy sake I may lay down my life with patience and joy. Amen![9]

For John Huss and for Paul, and even for each of us, such suffering is a choice we make. That is not to say we can choose to avoid pain but rather that we may select the reasons for our suffering. One writer described the process this way:

From the shedding of blood that initiates birth to the last gasp of astonishment in the face of death, we are encircled in suffering. The biography of a human being is also a history of anguish. The way one reacts to the suffering of life matters more, in creative and human terms, than the suffering itself. We become the people we are through the disadvantages and conflicts we prefer to more comfortable alternatives.[10]

On several occasions I have had the privilege of talking with Josef Tson. Josef was the pastor of the largest Baptist church in Romania during the days when the communists ruled his country. In 1973 he published a document that described how the communist government had obstructed religious freedom in his land. As the result of his brave disclosure, he was singled out for persecution and harassment. On one occasion, they threatened him with torture and death. This was his courageous response:

Your supreme weapon is killing. My supreme weapon is dying. Here is how it works. You know that my sermons on tape have spread all over the country. If you kill me, these sermons will be sprinkled with my blood. Everyone will know I died for my preaching.... So, sir, my sermons will speak ten times louder than before.

I will actually rejoice in this supreme victory if you kill me.[11]

COURAGE TO EMULATE PAUL

Paul realized that suffering was no longer an abstract term for the Philippians. Many of them had seen him suffer when the church at Philippi had been started. There he had been hounded by a demon-possessed girl, slandered, mobbed, stripped, beaten, and thrown into a dungeon. The courage these Philippians would need in the future was the kind they had observed in Paul during his adversity. I am certain some of the readers of this letter wondered if they would be brave enough to stand when their time came.

In calling this persecution "conflict," Paul used the word from which we get our word *agony*. It described the strenuous struggles of athletic contests. Paul employed the same word in his charge to Timothy: "Fight the good fight [*agona*] of faith" (1 Tim. 6:12). At the end of his life, Paul wrote, "I have fought the good fight [*agona*]" (2 Tim. 4:7).

Paul believed that persecution would be the lot of the believer until the end and that "we must through many tribulations enter the kingdom of God" (Acts 14:22). But he also encourages us with the promise that "the sufferings of this present time are not worthy to be compared with the glory which shall be revealed in us" (Rom. 8:18). In fact, he says that rather than being a setback, suffering is a stepping-stone. "If we endure, we shall also reign with Him. If we deny Him, He also will deny us" (2 Tim. 2:12).

It is often very difficult for us to maintain a positive attitude when adversity and pressures prevail. Paul wanted the trying circumstances to spur these believers on to greater victory and joy.

Some of the world's greatest men and women have been saddled with disabilities and adversities, but they have managed to overcome them and go on to greatness. They teach us that circumstances do not make us what we are but reveal what we are, as this illustration conveys:

> Cripple him, and you have a Sir Walter Scott. Lock him in a prison cell, and you have a John Bunyan. Bury him in the snows of Valley Forge, and you have a George Washington. Raise him in abject poverty, and you have an Abraham Lincoln. Subject him to bitter religious prejudice, and you have a Benjamin Disraeli. Strike him down with infantile paralysis, and he becomes a Franklin D. Roosevelt. Burn him so severely in a schoolhouse fire that the doctors say he will never walk again, and you have a Glenn Cunningham, who set a world's record in 1934 for running a mile in 4 minutes, 6.7 seconds. Deafen a genius composer, and you have Ludwig von Beethoven. Have him or her born black in a society filled with racial discrimination, and you have a Booker T. Washington, a Harriet Tubman, a Marian Anderson, or a George Washington Carver. Make

him the first child to survive in a poor Italian family of eighteen children, and you have Enrico Caruso. Have him born of parents who survived a Nazi concentration camp, paralyze him from the waist down when he is four, and you have an incomparable concert violinist, Itzhak Perlman. Call him a slow learner, "retarded," and write him off as ineducable, and you have an Albert Einstein.[12]

As I read Paul's words to the Philippians, I am reminded of a famous speech that was given by the sixty-five-year-old Winston Churchill as the Germans were about to invade England. The English were undermanned, ill-prepared, and poorly armed. The experts predicted Hitler's success would take but a few short weeks. The predictions of the experts would no doubt have come true had it not been for the powerful influence of Churchill's leadership. Here, in part, is what he said:

> The Battle of France is over. I expect that the Battle of Britain is about to begin. Upon this battle depends the survival of Christian civilization. The whole fury and might of the enemy must very soon be turned on us. Hitler knows that he will have to break us on this island or lose the war....
>
> Let us therefore brace ourselves to our duties and so bear ourselves that, if the British Empire

and its Commonwealth last for a thousand years,
men will still say: "This was their finest hour."[13]

More than anything else, Paul wanted the Philippians to stand strong so that whether he was with them or absent from them, they would be triumphant in Christ.

Therefore if there is any consolation in Christ, if any comfort of love, if any fellowship of the Spirit, if any affection and mercy, fulfill my joy by being like-minded, having the same love, being of one accord, of one mind. Let nothing be done through selfish ambition or conceit, but in lowliness of mind let each esteem others better than himself. Let each of you look out not only for his own interests, but also for the interests of others.

Let this mind be in you which was also in Christ Jesus, who, being in the form of God, did not consider it robbery to be equal with God, but made Himself of no reputation, taking the form of a bondservant, and coming in the likeness of men. And being found in appearance as a man, He humbled Himself and became obedient to the point of death, even the death of the cross. Therefore God also has highly exalted Him and given Him the name which is above every name, that at the name of Jesus every knee should bow, of those in heaven, and of those on earth, and of those under the earth, and that every tongue should confess that Jesus Christ is Lord, to the glory of God the Father.

Philippians 2:1–11

THE JOY OF UNITY

Philippians 2:1–11

Fulfill my joy by being like-minded.... Let this mind
be in you which was also in Christ Jesus.

A little boy strutting through the backyard, baseball cap in place, toting ball and bat, was overheard talking to himself. "I'm the greatest hitter in the world." Then he tossed the ball into the air, swung at it, and missed. "Strike one!" Undaunted, he picked up the ball, threw it into the air, said to himself, "I'm the greatest baseball hitter ever," and swung at the ball again. Again he missed. "Strike two!" He paused a moment to examine his bat and ball carefully. Then a third time he threw the ball into the air. "I'm the greatest hitter who ever lived," he said. He swung the bat hard a third time. He cried out, "Wow! Strike three! What a pitcher! I'm the greatest pitcher in the world!"

I like the kid's attitude. I predict that he will go far, no matter what he chooses to do in life. His spirit reminds me of something I read about Thomas Edison:

> In December 1914, the great Edison laboratories in West Orange, New Jersey, were almost entirely destroyed by fire. In one night, Edison lost two million dollars' worth of equipment and the record of much of his life's work. Edison's son, Charles, ran frantically about trying to find his father. Finally he came upon him, standing near the fire, his face ruddy in the glow, his white hair blown by the winter winds. "My heart ached for him," Charles Edison said. "He was no longer young, and everything was being destroyed. He spotted me. 'Where's your mother?' he shouted. 'Find her. Bring her here. She'll never see anything like this again as long as she lives.'"
>
> The next morning, walking about the charred embers of so many of his hopes and dreams, the sixty-seven-year-old Edison said, "There is great value in disaster. All our mistakes are burned up. Thank God we can start anew."[1]

With an attitude like that, no wonder Edison's name is still prominent one hundred years later. I'm not about to recommend the Pollyanna philosophy championed by so many "positive attitude" gurus. But I am going to make the point that Paul the apostle was making here in Philippians 2. Our attitudes are important! In fact, they are more important than our actions, because they are the foundation upon which our actions are built.

Twice in verse 2 Paul mentioned the Philippians' minds. He exhorted them to be like-minded and of "one mind." In verse 5, which is the key to this section, he wrote, "Let this mind be in you which was also in Christ Jesus." In chapter 4 he described some wholesome values and commanded his readers to "meditate on these things" (v. 8). Obviously, Paul knew the importance of a proper attitude.

Most commentators believe that these first eleven verses of chapter 2 are Paul's attempt to deal with the friction that had grown up in the Philippian assembly. Later on, the apostle would speak of this division and identify the names of two women in the congregation who were at odds with each other. He had already admonished the Philippian Christians to "stand fast in one spirit, with one mind striving together for the faith of the gospel" (1:27). Now he encouraged them to form the habits that would promote such harmony.

The attitude that was needed by these young believers was one of submission and servanthood. If they learned to serve one another, they would not slander each other. Before he finished making his point, Paul presented the greatest example of servanthood in history as he vividly told of Christ's humiliation and exaltation. His goal throughout was for these Christians to think like Christ: "Let this mind be in you which was also in Christ Jesus."

One of the amazing things about this section of Paul's letter is that he actually linked his own joy to the proper unity and fellowship of the Philippian church. That may not seem worth mentioning until you remember Paul's circumstances. He was writing from prison. Think about that for a moment:

> If we were in prison, chained, guarded, unjustly accused, vilified by those who ought to be our friends, with no comforts and no guaranteed future, what would our joy be? Paul's was … the topic of unity. "I will need no further happiness," he says, "if only I can hear that you are a united church."[2]

THE REASONS FOR CHRISTIAN UNITY

In using the word *if* to introduce the four statements in verse 1, Paul was not casting doubt upon his own premise. This particular Greek construction is one that assumes the statement being made is true. In some ways it would be better to translate the phrase with the word *since*. These statements make a strong appeal for unity in the body.

REASON ONE: THE EXPERIENCE OF CHRIST'S LIFE

The word *consolation* is the Greek word *paraklesis*, which means "to draw alongside of one." It is in Christ that we have great incentive to be encouragers and to draw alongside one another. It was Christ who reached out to encourage us when we were needy. The testimony of His entire ministry is one of helping and encouraging others. His famous prayer of John 17 is a model of concern for others. When we have experienced Christ's life, we must share it with our brothers and sisters.

REASON TWO: THE EXAMPLE OF CHRIST'S LOVE

The love mentioned here is first of all the love that Christ has for His own. We have felt His love toward us, and now that love is shed abroad in our hearts by the Holy Spirit, which He has given to us. The word *comfort* seems to indicate a spoken word of encouragement. It is the word used in 1 Thessalonians 5:14 where we are told to "comfort the fainthearted." The word *fainthearted* comes from a Greek word that could be translated "little soul." Comfort the little soul. The servant of Christ who is expressing the attitude of unity will be looking for people to encourage. The motivation behind this is God's love. As one writer put it, "The reason why God's servants love creatures so much is that they see how much Christ loves them, and it is one of the properties of love to love what is loved by the person we love."[3]

REASON THREE: THE ENCOURAGEMENT OF CHRIST'S BODY

When Paul spoke of the fellowship of the Spirit, he was telling the Macedonian Christians about the unity they should experience because they were all indwelt by the Spirit of God. The Holy Spirit who dwells in each believer joins all of them together as one body and becomes the common denominator of God's family. No matter how great the diversity among God's people, there should always be unity because of the Holy Spirit who lives within each one. Paul's point is this: if you understand the nature of Christ's body, you will be motivated toward unity.

REASON FOUR: THE EXPRESSION OF CHRIST'S COMPASSION

There are two dimensions to the compassion of Christ. The King James Version renders this phrase as "bowels and mercies," using a term by which the Greeks referred to all the inner organs of a human being. Actually, *bowels* is the Greek word for *kidney* and is a euphemism for the core of a person's being. We would use the word *heart* instead of *kidney* and say, "He loved us from His heart."

The second aspect of this compassion is "mercies." This is a reference to our outward acts of love when we love someone from the heart. Because of the inward and outward compassion of our Lord for us, we must express that same concern for one another.

These four statements were meant to be incentives to the believers in Philippi. William Hendriksen's summary statement is very helpful as we get our bearings in this section:

The main thrust of what the apostle is saying is this: If then you receive any help or encouragement or comfort from your vital union with Christ, and if the love of Christ toward you does at all provide you with an incentive for action; if, moreover, you are at all rejoicing in the marvelous Spirit-fellowship and if you have any experience of the tender mercy and compassion of Christ, then prove your gratitude for all this by loving your brothers and sisters at home.[4]

THE REQUIREMENTS FOR CHRISTIAN UNITY

Having laid out the reasons for unity, Paul went on to define what unity is and how it should be expressed.

REQUIREMENT ONE: HARMONY

They must be *one in mind*. These believers were to be "like-minded" and to have "one mind." This has to do with agreement in doctrine and creed. They were to hold to the same creed and embrace the same tenets of truth that they had been taught from the very beginning. No matter what liberal, free-thinking theologians may say, there is no spiritual unity without doctrinal oneness. When it comes to fundamental doctrines, A. T. Robertson said Christians should be "like clocks that strike at the same moment."[5]

They must be *one in heart.* Christians are to have the same love, not loving the same things but possessing the same love. They are to show that God's love is flowing in them and through them.

They must be *one in soul.* The phrase "of one accord" literally means to have "joint souls." We are to be soul brothers, in harmony with all God's people!

REQUIREMENT TWO: HUMILITY

A new word appears in verse 3. The word *each* is a reminder that we have personal responsibility. Each one of us is responsible for the unity of the body. If we do not take ownership over our own spirits and dispositions, there will be no unity in the body.

Paul challenged each one that he or she was not to do anything "through selfish ambition or conceit." This is a warning against a competitive, selfish spirit. Selfish ambition is a work of the flesh, according to Galatians 5:19–20, and is behind the petty squabbles and fights in so many churches today. Conceit means an empty glory. Someone has said that it is like a balloon. The larger it stretches on the outside, the bigger the emptiness on the inside. This was the disease of the Pharisees, who spoke great, swelling words of pride about their relationship with God but lacked substance or reality. J. Oswald Sanders portrayed the offensive nature of this attitude when he wrote:

> Nothing is more distasteful to God than self-conceit. This first and fundamental sin in essence aims at enthroning self at the expense

> of God.... Pride is a sin of whose presence its
> victim is least conscious.... If we are honest,
> when we measure ourselves by the life of our
> Lord who humbled Himself even to death on
> a cross, we cannot but be overwhelmed with
> the tawdriness and shabbiness, and even the
> vileness, of our hearts.[6]

A believer is to govern his life in lowliness of mind as he esteems others better than himself. The word translated "lowliness of mind" was transformed by the impact of the Christian gospel. Before Christ came, that word was viewed as a negative character trait, for it was associated with weakness and cowardliness. When Christ came, He taught His disciples how to submit to one another out of love instead of fear. Lowliness became the seed of the Christian grace of humility.

Besides the Lord Jesus Christ, Paul himself stands out as one of the true examples of this humility. During his third missionary journey, he referred to himself as "the least of the apostles" (1 Cor. 15:9). Later, during his first Roman imprisonment, he described himself as "the least of all the saints" (Eph. 3:8). Toward the close of his life, he wrote to Timothy and confessed that he considered himself the chief of sinners (1 Tim. 1:15). These were not statements of false piety but represented Paul's attitude toward himself as he viewed the totality of the body of Christ. There was no pride or arrogance about his many accomplishments. He truly considered others better than himself.

Gary Inrig tells about a well-known businessman who once demonstrated the ugliness of a boastful spirit in a public church service:

> As a matter of courtesy [he] was asked to bring a word of greeting. Unfortunately, he got rather carried away in the process and went on to tell the congregation about all the wonderful things he had done for the Lord. "I have a large house, a fine family, a successful business, and a good reputation. I have enough money to do whatever I want, and I am able to support some Christian ministries very generously, and many organizations want me to be a director. I have health and almost unlimited opportunities. Most people would love to change places with me. What more could God give me?" As he paused for effect, a voice shouted from the back of the auditorium, "How about a good dose of humility?"[7]

If there is to be unity in the church, the attitude of each individual will have to be one of humility. Each member will cultivate a measured opinion of himself. While he will readily acknowledge that God has given him a gift, he will not think more highly of himself than he ought to think. His attitude will not be one of overestimation or self-degradation but of proper appreciation.

REQUIREMENT THREE: HELPFULNESS

The final prerequisite for unity is an attitude of helpfulness. If a Christian values his brother highly and is practicing the spirit of humble-mindedness, he will naturally be looking for ways to help others. In Paul's words, he will not be looking out for his own interests but rather for the interests of others.

Peter Drucker, while not a spokesman for the evangelical faith, followed the biblical pattern when he wrote these words in his well-known management book *The Effective Executive*:

> The man who focuses on efforts and who stresses his downward authority is a subordinate no matter how exalted his title and rank. But the man who focuses on contribution and who takes responsibility for results, no matter how junior, is in the most literal sense of the phrase, "top management."[8]

If we care about unity, we do not approach a situation with the question, "What is in this for me? What will I get out of it?" Instead we ask, "What are the needs of others? What will benefit their growth? What can I do to help them?"

Nothing is more out of step with this than the fixation on self, which reigns in our culture today. Paul Vitz, in his book *Psychology as Religion*, explains the difference:

> It should be obvious—though it has apparently not been so to many—that the relentless and

single-minded search for and glorification of the self is at direct cross-purposes with the Christian injunction to lose the self. Certainly Jesus Christ neither lived nor advocated a life that would qualify by today's standards as "self-actualized." For the Christian, the self is the problem, not the potential paradise. Understanding this problem involves an awareness of sin, especially the sin of pride; correcting this condition requires the practice of such unself-actualized states as contrition and penitence, humility, obedience, and trust in God.[9]

So far we have explored the reasons for Christian unity:

- Reason one—the experience of Christ's life
- Reason two—the example of Christ's love
- Reason three—the encouragement of Christ's body
- Reason four—the expression of Christ's compassion

We have also investigated the requirements for Christian unity:

- Requirement one—harmony
- Requirement two—humility
- Requirement three—helpfulness

And now we come to the heart of this text.

THE ROLE MODEL FOR CHRISTIAN UNITY: JESUS CHRIST

In verses 5–11, we are exposed to the perfect role model for unity in the church. Dr. F. B. Meyer wrote of this section, "In the whole range of Scripture, this paragraph stands in almost unapproachable and unexampled majesty."[10] Most scholars agree that these verses are a hymn or poem that Paul either wrote himself or included here as an appropriate illustration. It provides a powerful conclusion to his message on unity.

While the story of the cross is recorded in the Gospels and explained in the Epistles, it is only in this passage that the Crucifixion is seen through the eyes of Christ Himself. We are given this glimpse of His perspective so that we might see the price that must be paid for unity—nothing less than death. It is a willingness to turn totally away from our own prerogatives in order that we might focus on the needs of others. No one has ever done that like Jesus Christ did. While the beauty of the Incarnation of our Savior is eloquently expressed in this paragraph, we must remember that this was not given as a doctrinal treatise. Rather, it is an illustration of the kind of humility and servanthood necessary to preserve unity in the body of Christ. Today's preachers use practical illustrations to explain doctrinal points; Paul used doctrine to explain the practical. Paul S. Rees correctly observed,

> The occasion and meaning of this eloquent out-
> burst are simple and clear. "Don't forget," cries

Paul, "that in all this wide universe and in all the dim reaches of history there has never been such a demonstration of self-effacing humility as when the Son of God in sheer grace descended to this errant planet! Remember that never—never in a million æons—would He have done it if He were the kind of Deity who looks 'only to His own interests' and closes His eyes to the 'interests of others!' You must remember, my brethren, that through your union with Him, in living, redemptive experience, this principle and passion by which He was moved must become the principle and passion by which you are moved."[11]

In order to feel the strength of Paul's hymn, let us look at each step that was involved for our Lord as He made the round-trip journey from glory to glory.

STEP ONE: HE RELINQUISHED HIS PLACE

Here are the words of the apostle to describe the place of prominence that Christ enjoyed: "Who, being in the form of God, did not consider it robbery to be equal with God" (Phil. 2:6). Phillips translated it this way: "For he, who had always been God by nature, did not cling to his prerogatives as God's equal."

If anyone had the right to be self-centered, it was Jesus Christ. He had existed throughout eternity. The word used here for "being" occurs fifty-nine times in the New Testament, and every time it has reference to prior existence. If we are to understand the greatness of Christ's sacrifice, we must try to comprehend the lofty position He held before He was made man. Not only had Christ existed eternally, but He had existed eternally as God.

Paul said that Christ existed "in the form of God." This phrase is not a reference to the outer appearance of Christ but indicates a profound and genuine inner identity. Jesus Christ was not simply *like* God; He was the very *nature* and *substance* of God. All that God is, Jesus Christ was and is and ever will be. To say that Jesus was in the form of God is the same as saying that Jesus was God.

Once in a while you might meet someone who will try to convince you that the Bible does not teach that Jesus is God. But the Bible consistently affirms what Paul was telling the Philippians:

> No one has seen God at any time. The only begotten Son, who is in the bosom of the Father, He has declared Him. (John 1:18)

> Jesus said ... "He who has seen Me has seen the Father." (John 14:9)

> He is the image of the invisible God, the firstborn over all creation. (Col. 1:15)

> For it pleased the Father that in Him [Christ] all the fullness should dwell. (Col. 1:19)

And without controversy great is the mystery
of godliness: God was manifested in the flesh.
(1 Tim. 3:16)

God … has in these last days spoken to us by His
Son … who being the brightness of His glory and
the express image of His person. (Heb. 1:1–3)

STEP TWO: HE REFUSED HIS PREROGATIVE

When the text says that Christ "did not consider it robbery to be
equal with God," it means He did not grasp or hold on to the outer
manifestation of His deity. He did not consider equality with God
a thing to be grasped. He did not view it as something to hold
on to at all costs. While we may not be able to fully understand
this, we do know that Christ surrendered *that* which He loved in
order that He might serve *those* whom He loved. Robert Gromacki
draws a straight line from the illustration to the dynamic truth that
stands behind it:

When Christ did not esteem His equality with
God as a prized possession, He did not look "on
his own things" (2:4). Instead, He viewed "the
things of others," namely, the sinful plight of
the human race. He did not contemplate what
He would gain for Himself, but rather what He
could do for others.[12]

Please do not miss your role in all this. Jesus made a choice to become a servant! Verse 7 says, "[He] made Himself of no reputation." Verse 8 says, "He humbled Himself." In both cases the reflexive expression is used to denote a very pointed personal decision. If the only person in the world who ever had the right to assert His rights waived them, then you and I can do the same!

STEP THREE: HE RENOUNCED HIS PRIVILEGES

He was by His very nature God, but the text says He "made Himself of no reputation." Some versions translate this, "He emptied Himself." The word *emptied* in the Greek, *kenoō*, means "to deprive something of its proper place and use." J. B. Phillips translated the phrase this way: "[He] stripped himself of all privilege."

Many have attempted to explain the self-emptying of Christ by saying that when He came to earth, He laid aside His deity. But no real student of the Scriptures believes that His self-emptying was a diminishing of His deity. Deity, once diminished, is no longer deity! Others have suggested that Christ's self-emptying involved divesting Himself of the relative attributes of deity—omniscience, omnipresence, and omnipotence—while keeping the essential attributes of holiness, love, and righteousness. This idea robs Jesus Christ of the substance necessary for His Saviorhood. If He in any manner ceased to be God, He is disqualified to be the redeemer of sinful man.

A. T. Robertson explained it this way: "Of what did Christ empty Himself? Not of His divine nature. That was impossible. He continued to be the Son of God.... Undoubtedly, Christ gave up His environment of glory."[13]

The best and most accurate way to define the self-emptying of Jesus is that, in His incarnation, Christ voluntarily surrendered the independent exercise of His divine attributes. He never ceased to possess them all, but He voluntarily put Himself under the authority of God the Father and under the control of the Holy Spirit in their exercise. There is no record of Jesus having used these divine attributes in His first thirty years of human existence, but when the Spirit came upon Him at His baptism, He began to demonstrate these powers.

STEP FOUR: HE RESTRICTED HIS PRESENCE

One of the most overlooked aspects of our Lord's coming to earth is the restriction that it placed on His presence. When we read of Christ "taking the form of a bondservant, and coming in the likeness of men," do we understand that Jesus gave up His unbounded universal freedom, instead being confined in a human body that in turn was confined to a country no bigger than Palestine?

When we are told that Jesus took the *form* of a bondservant, the same word is employed that describes Jesus as being in the *form* of God. Jesus was in the *form of God* and He took upon Himself the *form of a bondservant.* His servanthood was authentic in substance and reality.

Hebrews says that "though He was a Son, yet He learned obedience by the things which He suffered" (5:8). Jesus affirmed His slave status on numerous occasions. To His disciples He said, "I am among you as the One who serves," and "The Son of Man did not come to be served, but to serve, and to give His life a ransom for many" (Luke 22:27; Matt. 20:28).

Paul's statement here about the Incarnation is that Jesus was "in the likeness of men." The word *likeness* suggests similarity but difference. Though His humanity was genuine, He was different from all other humans in that He was sinless. Paul told the Romans that God sent forth His own Son "in the likeness of sinful flesh" (Rom. 8:3).

I have always been impressed with the words that are used in the New Testament to describe our Lord's entrance into the human realm. He "became flesh" (John 1:14); He was "born of a woman" (Gal. 4:4); He was "born of the seed of David according to the flesh" (Rom. 1:3); He was "manifested in the flesh" (1 Tim. 3:16); He "shared in the same [flesh and blood]" (Heb. 2:14); He came "in the flesh" (1 John 4:2–3; 2 John 7). His time on earth is referred to as "the days of His flesh" (Heb. 5:7).

If you wonder what it must have been like for God to become a man, perhaps C. S. Lewis can help:

> Did you ever think, when you were a child, what fun it would be if your toys could come to life? Well suppose you could really have brought them to life. Imagine turning a tin soldier into a real little man. It would involve turning the tin into flesh. And suppose the tin soldier did not like it.

He is not interested in flesh: all he sees is that the tin is being spoilt. He thinks you are killing him. He will do everything he can to prevent you. He will not be made into a man if he can help it.

What you would have done about that tin soldier I do not know. But what God did about us was this. The Second Person in God, the Son, became human Himself: was born into the world as an actual man—a real man of a particular height, with hair of a particular colour, speaking a particular language, weighing so many stone. The Eternal Being, who knows everything and who created the whole universe, became not only a man but (before that) a baby, and before that a *foetus* inside a Woman's body. If you want to get the hang of it, think how you would like to become a slug or a crab.[14]

STEP FIVE: HE REALIZED HIS PURPOSE

The death of Jesus Christ was not an accident. It was in the program of God from before the foundation of the world. Nearly one-third of the material in the Gospels is devoted to His days in the shadow of the cross, because the very purpose for His coming was His death. "Even the Son of Man did not come to be served, but to serve, and to give His life a ransom for many" (Mark 10:45).

The writer of the book of Hebrews made it very clear that our Lord was made man for one supreme reason:

But we see Jesus, who was made a little lower than the angels, for the suffering of death … that He, by the grace of God, might taste death for everyone. (2:9)

Inasmuch then as the children have partaken of flesh and blood, He Himself likewise shared in the same, that through death He might destroy him who had the power of death, that is, the devil. (2:14)

Therefore, when He came into the world, He said: … "A body You have prepared for Me." … Then He said, "Behold, I have come to do Your will, O God." … By that will we have been sanctified through the offering of the body of Jesus Christ once for all. (10:5, 9–10)

And now at last, in Paul's illustration of unity, we are taken to the very purpose for Christ's coming: "He humbled Himself and became obedient to the point of death, even the death of the cross" (Phil. 2:8).

During some unsettled days in ancient Rome, a slave heard that his master's name was on the liquidation list. He quickly put on his master's cloak and quietly awaited the arrival of the political butchers. When they found the slave dressed in his master's clothing, they killed him, supposing him to be the master. Likewise, the Master of the universe, Jesus Christ, took on Himself the cloak of our humanity. The death He endured is the death we deserved. Through His death, we have been spared.

When our Lord's death is described by the phrase "even the death of the cross," we are reminded of the terrible punishment He endured on our behalf. Crucifixion was reserved for non-Romans and terrible criminals. A person who was crucified died a thousand deaths before finally dying. For Christ it was all that physical suffering and much more:

> From below, Satan and all his hosts assailed Him.
> From round about men heaped scorn upon Him,
> from above, God dropped upon Him the pallor
> of darkness, symbol of the curse; and from within
> there arose the bitter cry, "My God, My God,
> why hast Thou forsaken Me?" Into this hell, this
> hell of Calvary, Christ descended.[15]

STEP SIX: HE RECEIVED HIS PROMOTION

This great doctrinal passage is a systematic Christology. Here we learn of Christ's preexistence, His incarnation, His humiliation, His crucifixion, and now His ascension and exaltation. The ascension of Christ at the end of forty days is clearly documented by Luke in Acts 1:9–11.

Liberal scholars like to say the Ascension was just a story told to express the way the church felt about Jesus at the time of His death. But Luke's record is an eyewitness account of the ascension of our Lord into heaven. In fact, Luke employed five different terms for "sight" to assure the historicity of this event. We are told that the disciples "watched," that He was "taken up … out of their sight," that they "looked steadfastly toward heaven as He went up," that the angels asked them why they were "gazing up into heaven," and that they were told that the same Jesus would return to earth in like manner "as you saw Him go into heaven."

The Ascension was the beginning of His exaltation, for Christ is now seated at the right hand of the Father in heaven. Paul looked beyond this day, however, to a yet future day when every knee will be made to bow before Him and every tongue will be caused to confess that He is Lord to the glory of God the Father. At the mere mention of His name, everyone above the earth will bow, including all the good angels and all the redeemed who have died before Christ returns. Everyone on the earth will bow, including all human beings. Everyone under the earth will bow, including all the inhabitants of hell and all the evil angels. And in that moment, the cycle will have been completed. The One who was humiliated will be exalted. The One who was brought low will be raised up high.

By His life, Jesus teaches us that the way up is the way down. Peter put it this way: "Therefore humble yourselves under the mighty hand of God, that He may exalt you in due time" (1 Pet. 5:6). James said, "Humble yourselves in the sight of the Lord, and He will lift you up" (4:10).

Three times in His ministry Jesus spoke on the text: "Whoever exalts himself will be humbled, and he who humbles himself will be exalted" (Matt. 23:12; Luke 14:11; 18:14).

Since Christ humbled Himself, we must be willing to humble ourselves, and as we continue to live in humble obedience to His will, we can anticipate our moment of exaltation some future day!

Therefore, my beloved, as you have always obeyed,
not as in my presence only, but now much more
in my absence, work out your own salvation with
fear and trembling; for it is God who works in
you both to will and to do for His good pleasure.

Do all things without complaining and disputing,
that you may become blameless and harmless,
children of God without fault in the midst of a
crooked and perverse generation, among whom you
shine as lights in the world, holding fast the word
of life, so that I may rejoice in the day of Christ
that I have not run in vain or labored in vain.

Philippians 2:12–16

5

THE JOY OF RESPONSIBILITY

Philippians 2:12–16

Work out your own salvation with fear and trembling.

I have always thought the most important single ingredient to success in athletics or in life is discipline. I have many times felt that this word is the most ill-defined in all our language. My favorite definition of the word is as follows:

1. Do what has to be done.
2. Do it when it has to be done.
3. Do it as well as it can be done.
4. Do it that way all the time.[1]

It probably won't surprise you to learn that I have written these words in the flyleaf of my Bible. What will surprise you, if you are not an avid follower of basketball, is the identity of the author. His name is Bob Knight, the former US Olympic basketball coach, a member of the Basketball Hall of Fame, and the former coach of the Indiana University Hoosiers and the Texas Tech Red Raiders. While there is much about Bobby Knight's lifestyle that troubles me, I think his definition of discipline is one of the best I have ever read.

Forrest Gregg, former NFL player and coach, said the same thing in a different way: "I believe in discipline. You can forgive incompetence. You can forgive lack of ability. But one thing you cannot ever forgive is lack of discipline."[2] The legendary Tom Landry added, "Setting a goal is not the main thing. It is deciding how you will go about achieving it and staying with that plan. The key is discipline. Without it there is no morale."[3]

R. Kent Hughes, in his book *Disciplines of a Godly Man*, tells about the regimen of former Chicago Bears defensive linebacker Mike Singletary:

> Those who have watched Mike Singletary … "play" … are usually surprised when they meet him. He is not an imposing hulk. He is barely six feet tall and weighs, maybe, 220. Whence the greatness? *Discipline*. Mike Singletary is as disciplined a student of the game as any who have ever played it.… In watching game films he will often run a single play fifty to sixty times.… It takes him three hours to watch half a football game, which is only twenty to thirty plays! Because he watches every

player, because he mentally knows the opposition's tendency … because he reads the opposition's mind through their stances, he is often moving toward the ball's preplanned destination before the play develops. Mike Singletary's legendary success is testimony to his remarkably disciplined life.[4]

Merriam-Webster's Collegiate Dictionary lists as one definition of *discipline* "training that corrects, molds, or perfects the mental faculties or moral character."[5] This was the burden on Paul's heart as he continued his letter to the Philippians. He was going to hold them responsible to discipline their own moral character until it fell in line with the "mind of Christ," which he so fervently described in the first eleven verses of this chapter.

When he began this section with the word *therefore*, he was obviously connecting it to that which had gone before. Christ disciplined Himself to obey His Father, even when it meant going to the cross. That same discipline of obedience is now to be practiced in the lives of those who call themselves Christians. Christ was obedient in death; they must be obedient in life. Bishop Handley Moule made the connection:

> We have still in our ears the celestial music … of the great paragraph of the incarnation … the journey of the Lord of love from glory to glory by way of the awful cross. May we not now give ourselves awhile wholly to reverie, and feast upon

the divine poetry at our leisure? Not so; the immediate sequel is that we are to be holy. We are to act in the light and wonder of so vast an act of love, in the wealth and resource of so great a salvation. We are to set spiritually to work.[6]

As Paul moved from doctrine to practice, he explained three disciplines that need to be developed. Maybe the best way for us to personalize them is to express them as resolutions.

DISCIPLINE ONE: I WILL DO MY PART

When the text says, "Work out your own salvation," it does not mean "work *for* your salvation." That should be obvious to us since we have already identified the readers of the letter as "the saints in Christ Jesus." The phrase "work out" has the meaning of working something through to its full completion. This particular expression was used to describe those who worked in the mines of Paul's day. They were mining out of the ground that which had been placed there by their Creator. Working out our salvation has the meaning of working out what God has already worked in.

The New Testament is very clear about the nature of salvation. It is not the result of man's efforts but comes through the grace of God. I have noticed, however, that in many of the passages where the doctrine of salvation *apart from works* is found, the doctrine of salvation *unto good works* is also found. Here are three examples:

For by grace you have been saved through faith, and that not of yourselves; it is the gift of God, not of works, lest anyone should boast. For we are His workmanship, created in Christ Jesus for good works, which God prepared beforehand that we should walk in them. (Eph. 2:8–10)

Not by works of righteousness which we have done, but according to His mercy He saved us, through the washing of regeneration and renewing of the Holy Spirit.... This is a faithful saying, and these things I want you to affirm constantly, that those who have believed in God should be careful to maintain good works. These things are good and profitable to men. (Titus 3:5, 8)

Who gave Himself for us, that He might redeem us from every lawless deed and purify for Himself His own special people, zealous for good works. (Titus 2:14)

Who really is responsible for a believer's spiritual growth? In the late 1800s Bishop J. C. Ryle was asking this question:

Is it wise to proclaim in so bald, naked, and unqualified a way as many do, that the holiness of converted people is by faith only, and not at all by personal exertion? Is it according to the proportion of God's Word? I doubt it. That faith in Christ is the root of all holiness … no well-instructed Christian will ever think of denying. But surely the Scriptures teach us that in following holiness the true Christian needs personal exertion and work as well as faith.[7]

While each generation of believers carries on its own debate over this question, the Bible holds the tension between man's role and God's role in perfect balance. Here's an illustration from the book of 2 Peter, where Peter reminded his readers that they had been given "all things that pertain to life and godliness" (1:3). He added to their stockpile of resources the "exceedingly great and precious promises" (v. 4). But having inventoried their spiritual assets, Peter did not encourage a passive attitude toward the Christian life. He was not telling these scattered believers that since they had all these things, they need not be involved in the process of their maturity. On the contrary, the very next verses read, "For this very reason, giving all diligence, add to your faith virtue, to virtue knowledge, to knowledge self-control, to self-control perseverance, to perseverance godliness, to godliness brotherly kindness, and to brotherly kindness love" (vv. 5–7).

What Peter was saying to his readers is exactly what Paul had written to the Philippians: "You have been given great resources; now go out and realize the full potential of all that you are and have in Christ Jesus."

Perhaps you have noticed that today there seems to be a movement away from personal discipline and individual responsibility in the Christian walk. In one of his excellent Navigator books, Jerry Bridges wrote:

> We Christians may be very disciplined and industrious in our business, our studies, our home, or even our ministry, but we tend to be lazy when it comes to exercise in our own spiritual lives. We would much rather pray, "Lord, make me godly," and expect Him to "pour" some godliness into our souls in some mysterious way. God does in fact work in a mysterious way to make us godly, but He does not do this apart from the fulfillment of our own personal responsibility. We are to train ourselves to be godly.[8]

Jay Adams pointed his finger at the same root cause when he observed:

> You may have sought and tried to obtain instant godliness. There is no such thing. We want somebody to give us three easy steps to godliness, and we'll take them next Friday and be godly. The trouble is, godliness doesn't come that way.[9]

When Paul wrote to young Timothy to instruct him in his Christian growth, he gave him the secret to godliness that he had learned through many years of study and practice: "Reject profane and old wives' fables, and exercise yourself toward godliness" (1 Tim. 4:7). The word translated "exercise" comes from the Greek word *gumnos*, from which we get our word *gymnasium*. This command of Paul has the smell of the Olympic Games all over it. He told his disciple that the godly life would come only through spiritual sweat.

This discipline of personal responsibility was to take an even higher priority in Paul's absence than it did in his presence. This is the second time in this letter that he made this particular point:

> Only let your conduct be worthy of the gospel of Christ, so that whether I come and see you or am absent, I may hear of your affairs, that you stand fast in one spirit, with one mind striving together for the faith of the gospel. (Phil. 1:27)

> Therefore, my beloved, as you have always obeyed, not as in my presence only, but now much more in my absence, work out your own salvation with fear and trembling. (2:12)

Of this, William Hendriksen wrote:

> The obedience of the Philippians must not be motivated by, and last only as long as, Paul's

> presence among them. On the contrary, his very
> absence must impress upon them the fact that
> now more than ever they must take the initiative.
> Now especially they must exert themselves, for
> now they are on their own. They must work out
> "their own salvation" … apart from the assistance
> of Paul.[10]

The importance of this responsibility is underscored by the instruction to carry it out "with fear and trembling" (Eph. 6:5). Phillips translated it this way: "With a proper sense of respect and responsibility." On several other occasions, Paul used this same expression. He told the Corinthians that he ministered the word to them in fear and trembling (1 Cor. 2:3). He reminded the Corinthians that they had received Titus with "fear and trembling" (2 Cor. 7:15). He wrote to the Ephesians that they were to obey their masters with "fear and trembling" (6:5).

No matter how we may wish to explain these instructions, one thing is certain: Paul took the responsibility of the believer very seriously. They were not to enter into this process with a relaxed and easy attitude. The temptation of the world and the devious strategies of the Devil demanded a sober approach to their Christian growth.

DISCIPLINE TWO: I WILL DEPEND ON GOD

There is one worker in Philippians 2:12 and another worker in verse 13. The Christian is working out his own salvation in verse 12.

God is working in the Christian in verse 13. We are to work because He has already worked. All *we* can do is respond to what *He* has done. Kenneth S. Wuest accurately translated this phrase, "For God is the One who is constantly putting forth His power in you."[11] In one of his benedictions Paul said, "Now to Him who is able to do exceedingly abundantly above all that we ask or think, according to the power that works in us" (Eph. 3:20).

God has worked in us. He is working in us. He will continue to work in us. We are to work diligently so that we might realize the benefit of all that God has done and is doing for us. Both divine enablement and human responsibility are involved.

One of my favorite illustrations of this cooperative partnership between God and man is the story of a farmer who was once visited by his pastor. As the pastor surveyed the farm for the first time, he commented, "John, this is a great farm you and God have!" "Thank you," said John. "But you should have seen it when God had it all by Himself."

The farmer meant no disrespect. He was simply acknowledging the way God works—through us. He will not do for us what we should be doing ourselves. As we cooperate with Him, we can see the potential of our Christian lives realized.

Two infinitives are used to describe what God does—"to will" and "to do." Both the desire and the deed belong to God. Both the prompting and the performing belong to God. Paul expressed that thought to the Corinthian believers in this way: "I labored more abundantly than they all, yet not I, but the grace of God which was with me" (1 Cor. 15:10).

F. B. Meyer helps me understand how this arrangement really works:

> He may be working in you to confess to that fellow Christian that you were unkind in your speech or act. Work it out. He may be working in you to give up that line of business about which you have been doubtful lately. Give it up. He may be working in you to be sweeter in your home, and gentler in your speech. Begin. He may be working in you to alter your relations with some with whom you have dealings that are not as they should be. Alter them. This very day let God begin to speak, and work and will; and then work out what He works in. God will not work apart from you, but He wants to work through you. Let Him. Yield to Him, and let this be the day when you shall begin to live in the power of the mighty Indwelling One.[12]

DISCIPLINE THREE: I WILL BE DIFFERENT FROM THE WORLD

Many who have written on the book of Philippians have commented on the contrast between the end of verse 13 and the beginning of verse 14. In verse 13 we are told that it is God who does the work. Then, without so much as a transition sentence, we are instructed, "Do all things." Here is a vivid illustration of the principle we have already discussed. God is working, and we are to be working as well.

When we are obedient to do all that we know God wants of us, then we have the joy of entering into all that God is doing in us.

It would be unlike Paul to leave such an important doctrinal concept without giving some advice as to how this principle works in everyday life. Notice how very contemporary his illustrations appear! As Christians we must live in the world, but there should be a noticeable difference in our lifestyle. They murmur and complain and gripe, but we should not. They live according to a crooked standard and a corrupt ethic, but we are to be harmless and blameless. They inhabit the darkness, but we are to shine as lights. They hold out empty hands to an empty generation, but we offer the word of life.

CHEERFUL LIVING IN AN UNHAPPY WORLD

Paul instructed the Philippians to "do all things without [murmuring] and disputing." Dwight Pentecost defined *murmuring* as an "outward expression of an inner lawlessness and rebellion that shakes the fist in the face of God and repudiates His right to rule, that questions His love and His wisdom."[13]

The word *murmuring* comes from a Greek word that means "to mutter or to grumble." The children of Israel had turned murmuring into an Olympic sport. They murmured at the Red Sea when they saw the chariots of the Egyptians coming after them (Exod. 14:10–12). They murmured at Marah, where the waters were bitter (15:22–24). They murmured in the wilderness when they had no food (16:3). They murmured at Rephidim, where they had no water (17:1–3). They murmured at Kadesh Barnea because the spies reported the presence of giants in the land (Num. 13:31–14:2).

Moses told them their complaining was really an attack upon the goodness of God: "Your [murmurings] are not against us but against the LORD" (Exod. 16:8). Paul used these experiences of the Israelites to exhort the believers in Corinth. He wrote, "Nor [murmur], as some of them also [murmured], and were destroyed by the destroyer" (1 Cor. 10:10).

It is said of Daniel Webster that when he wanted to give a person the impression that he remembered him when he could not recall his name or where they had met before, he used a simple device. He would simply ask, "How's the old complaint?" Nine times out of ten the technique worked. The person would begin to unfold some grievance that he had discussed with Mr. Webster on a former occasion, and sooner or later he would thereby identify himself.

Webster's technique should never work with Christians. They are to do all things without murmuring. Paul knew that before the Christians in Philippi could make an impact on their city, they had to straighten out the problems in their own assembly. They could not be grumbling and complaining among themselves and at the same time be attracting people to Christ!

Murmuring is one of those words that sounds like its meaning. The term for words such as *hiss*, *buzz*, or *hum* is *onomatopoeia*. Such words have the sound of the things they represent.

Grumbling or complaining is an outward activity that grows out of the inward spirit of disputing or questioning. Disputing is not the same as disagreeing, however. In his ministry, Paul openly disagreed with Barnabas, Peter, and the men of Jerusalem. It is the old story of being able to disagree without being disagreeable!

STRAIGHT LIVING IN A CROOKED WORLD

The challenge to live blamelessly is a call to live above reproach before believers and unbelievers alike. To live blamelessly is to live with integrity, so that no one can point an accusing finger.

The word *harmless* means "pure or unmixed." It was used to describe wine that had not been diluted or gold jewelry that was without alloy. It is translated by the word *simple* in Romans 16:19, where Paul told the Romans that he wanted them to be "simple" concerning evil. Jesus used the word when He told the twelve disciples that they were to be harmless as doves (Matt. 10:16).

Such blameless and harmless conduct was to be lived out before a world that is described here as "crooked and perverse." When Paul described his world as "crooked," he used the Greek word *skolias*. It is from this word that we get the word *scoliosis*, which is the medical term for the curvature of the spine. When he added to this the descriptive term *perverse*, he was speaking of that which is *permanently* disfigured or distorted.

In the early nineties, James Patterson and Peter Kim offered us a glimpse of the kind of crookedness that makes up our American world. In a book titled *The Day America Told the Truth*, they recorded the results of an extensive survey that guaranteed the anonymity of the respondents. R. Kent Hughes summarized the results of their survey in these alarming paragraphs:

Only 13 percent of Americans see all Ten Commandments as binding on us today. Ninety-one percent lie regularly—at home and at work. In answer to the question, "Whom have you regularly lied to?" the statistics included 86 percent to parents and 75 percent to friends. A third of AIDS carriers admit to not having told their lovers. Most workers admit to goofing off for an average of seven hours—almost one whole day—a week, and half admit that they regularly call in sick when they are perfectly well.

The survey also posed the question, "What are you willing to do for $10 million?" Twenty-five percent would abandon their families, 23 percent would become a prostitute for a week, and 7 percent would kill a stranger. Think of it! In a gathering of 100 Americans, there are seven who would consider killing you if the price was right. In 1,000 there are seventy![14]

In 1992, *Newsweek* carried an article about a new book that had just hit our college campuses. The title of the book was *Cheating 101*. Here is part of the story:

Whoever said cheaters never prosper never met Michael Moore. A junior at New Jersey's Rutgers University, Moore is the author of *Cheating 101:*

The Benefits and Fundamentals of Earning the Easy A. An 87-page guide to academic guile, *Cheating* offers the finer points of plagiarizing, swiping exams and passing answers right under the professor's nose.... Moore really doesn't see himself as a Fagin or a fink. "I don't think I'm making a cheater out of anybody," he says. "It's their choice, like drunk driving. It's only wrong if you get caught."[15]

There is no better way to describe this generation than the word Paul used: *skolias* ... crooked! You can be sure the believer who walks straight will not get lost in the crowd!

RADIANT LIVING IN A DARK WORLD

In the midst of such a world, the believer is not to just exist; he is to shine forth as a light and offer others the hope of God's Word. The apostle John said that Jesus was "the light of men" (John 1:4). Jesus said, "As long as I am in the world, I am the light of the world" (9:5). When the Savior was speaking to His disciples, He said, "You are the light of the world" (Matt. 5:14). In that same context He commanded them, "Let your light so shine before men, that they may see your good works and glorify your Father in heaven" (v. 16). Paul reminded all Christians, "For you were once darkness, but now you are light in the Lord. Walk as children of light" (Eph. 5:8).

The sequence of Paul's directives is intentional. We must be blameless and harmless before we can shine forth as lights:

Light is a beautiful illustration of something that does what it has to do by being what it ought to be. It is therefore very appropriate in Paul's argument in these verses. Responsibility for the world around, outreach, making an impact, telling others about Jesus, these thoughts are entertained only after he has laid a foundation of Christian personal holiness. Like the light we must "be" if we are to "do."[16]

When we "shine as lights in the world," the testimony of our personal holiness makes an impact on those around us. But the testimony of a righteous lifestyle is incomplete if there is no explanation to accompany it. I never have believed too much in the power of the silent witness. But when a godly life is accompanied by the presentation of the word of life, the effect can be dramatic.

The word of life is the total message of God's Word. It not only brings life to those who are dead in their sins but it also sustains life each day for the disciple who is nurtured by it. When we are told to "hold it fast," the word that is used is one that was often chosen to describe a host offering wine to a guest at a banquet. It is the picture of a gracious offer of the gospel of Jesus Christ to those who do not know Him.

The disciplines of the Christian life were never meant to be easy. The Bible describes them as temptation (James 1:12), persecution (2 Cor. 4:9), sufferings (Rom. 8:18, 23), patient endurance (James 5:7–11), refining and perfecting (James 1:2–4), unceasing labor (1 Cor. 3:8–15), the good fight of faith (1 Tim. 6:12), and a struggle toward a goal that is beyond this world (Rom. 8:22). The only way to live such a life victoriously is to be constantly reminded of the goal! Paul was a master at keeping his goal in sight. Later on in this letter he wrote, "Reaching forward to those things which are ahead, I press toward the goal for the prize of the upward call of God in Christ Jesus" (3:13–14).

Already, on two occasions, he has mentioned the coming day of Christ (1:6, 10). It is evident that he lived continually with his eye on that day. He was no doubt thinking of that day when he wrote that he considered the Philippians to be his "joy and crown" (4:1). He wrote in a similar fashion to the Thessalonians, "For what is our hope, or joy, or crown of rejoicing? Is it not even you in the presence of our Lord Jesus Christ at His coming? For you are our glory and joy" (1 Thess. 2:19–20).

Now he told his beloved Philippians that he wanted them to live in such a way that he would be proud of them when he stood before Christ on that momentous day. He wanted to be able to look back and rejoice that his time with them was not spent in vain. If, on the day of Christ, these Philippians were standing with him, it would be the final evidence that all his effort and labor on their behalf was not wasted.

Jonathan Edwards, who lived in the early 1700s, was one of the key figures in the intellectual history of New England. He was converted at the age of seventeen and died from the effects of a smallpox injection at the young age of fifty-five. He is still widely read and admired for his intellectual prowess and godliness. One biographer sized up his life in this way:

Jonathan Edwards is important not only for his pastoral insight, personal saintliness, and commanding intellect; he is one of the very few in the history of the church who seems to have been granted an almost perfect integration of "the heart" and "the head."[17]

In no part of his life was that balance between head and heart more evident than in his disciplined commitment to personal holiness. More than most of his contemporaries, Jonathan Edwards believed that salvation and sanctification were wholly of God, but he also understood his own responsibility. He used to make resolutions. One of them was, "Resolved, never to do anything which I would be afraid to do if it were the last hour of my life."[18]

Like the apostle Paul, he lived a godly life with his eyes on the future.

Yes, and if I am being poured out as a drink offering on the
sacrifice and service of your faith, I am glad and rejoice with you
all. For the same reason you also be glad and rejoice with me.

But I trust in the Lord Jesus to send Timothy to you shortly,
that I also may be encouraged when I know your state. For
I have no one like-minded, who will sincerely care for your
state. For all seek their own, not the things which are of Christ
Jesus. But you know his proven character, that as a son with
his father he served with me in the gospel. Therefore I hope
to send him at once, as soon as I see how it goes with me. But
I trust in the Lord that I myself shall also come shortly.

Yet I considered it necessary to send to you Epaphroditus, my
brother, fellow worker, and fellow soldier, but your messenger
and the one who ministered to my need; since he was longing
for you all, and was distressed because you had heard that he
was sick. For indeed he was sick almost unto death; but God
had mercy on him, and not only on him but on me also, lest
I should have sorrow upon sorrow. Therefore I sent him the
more eagerly, that when you see him again you may rejoice,
and I may be less sorrowful. Receive him therefore in the Lord
with all gladness, and hold such men in esteem; because for
the work of Christ he came close to death, not regarding his
life, to supply what was lacking in your service toward me.

Philippians 2:17–30

THE JOY OF MINISTRY

Philippians 2:17–30

*If I am being poured out as a drink offering on the sacrifice
and service of your faith, I am glad and rejoice with you all.*

In 1924 at the Paris Olympic Games, Eric Liddell stirred his generation with his refusal to race on Sunday and his ultimate victory in the four-hundred-meter dash. The entire story was depicted in the Academy Award–winning film *Chariots of Fire*. If you saw the film, you will remember the surprise you felt when at the end you read these words about the hero of the film:

> Eric Liddell, missionary, died in occupied China at
> the end of World War II. All of Scotland mourned.

It was exactly one year after winning the gold medal that Eric Liddell went to China as a missionary with the London Missionary

Society. After teaching at a college there, he decided to engage in rural evangelism; by bicycle and by foot he carried the gospel of Jesus Christ to the backcountry of China.

After Japan invaded China and World War II broke out, Liddell was classified as an enemy national, and in August 1943 he was sent to a prison camp. He was one of 1,800 prisoners packed into a facility that measured 150 by 200 yards. He was housed in a dormitory that provided a room three feet by six feet for each man. While a prisoner, Liddell accepted the challenge of his situation and organized athletic meets, taught hymns, and ministered God's Word.

David Michell was a child who was interned along with Eric Liddell. He later remembered the influence this national hero had upon everyone in the prison. "None of us will ever forget this man who was totally committed to putting God first, a man whose humble life combined muscular Christianity with radiant godliness."[1]

Just months before he would have been liberated, on February 21, 1945, Eric Liddell died of a brain tumor. He was a national hero, but more than that he was a hero of the faith. His life and testimony continue to inspire others to follow Christ.

Eric Liddell is one of the few heroes to emerge in our century. Even though he lived and died before I was looking for a role model, I still profit from his life. But which young people can we look to today? Randy Alcorn laments this lack of positive role models:

> Much can be determined about a nation's ideals
> and future welfare by the character of its models.
> Who are the most admired people in America?

Spiritual leaders, civic leaders, altruistic social reformers? Hardly. The heroes and idols of America are actors and actresses, jetsetters and yacht owners, entertainers and rock stars. With a glass of wine or a joint in one hand, and somebody else's mate in the other, they prance, jiggle, curse, and swindle their way into the hearts of Americans. Our homage to such celebrities tells us as much about us—and our probable destiny—as it does them.[2]

In the introduction to his biography of the apostle Paul, J. Oswald Sanders relates this problem to the church with painful honesty:

Each generation has to meet and resolve its own leadership problems, and we today are facing an acute crisis in leadership.... The church has not escaped this dearth of authoritative leadership. Her voice, which once sounded a clarion call of hope to beleaguered humanity, is now strangely muted, and her influence in the world community has become minimal. The salt has largely lost its savor, and the light its radiance.[3]

I recently read that when Raphael was painting his famous Vatican frescoes, a couple of cardinals stopped by to watch and

COUNT IT ALL JOY

criticize. "The face of the apostle Paul is too red," said one. Raphael replied, "He blushes to see into whose hands the church has fallen."[4]

No one needs to remind us that we live in an age of fallen heroes. But maybe instead of spending so much time analyzing our failures, we ought to seek out some solid role models to emulate and then determine to become the same for the generation that is looking to us.

Paul introduced three such people in the last half of Philippians 2. We learn that *Paul* himself was an example of *selflessness*. Paul then presented his spiritual son *Timothy* as an example of *service*. Finally, we are introduced to *Epaphroditus* as an example of *suffering*. Paul was an apostle, Timothy was a pastor, and Epaphroditus was a layman. While it is true that Jesus Christ is the Christian's model, these men are presented as model Christians. Jesus poured Himself out in service to God. These men poured themselves out as servants of Jesus Christ.

PAUL: THE MODEL OF SELFLESSNESS

While six verses each are devoted to Timothy and Epaphroditus, only two verses are dedicated to describing Paul's attitude. It is amazing that in these two verses that discuss sacrifice, Paul used the words *glad* and *rejoice* and then repeated them. Just as Jesus lived out His life for the joy that was set before Him, so Paul was willing to endure hardship that he might know that same joy.

In this passage, the apostle was not pointing to himself and telling the Philippians to follow him, but he did do that on many other occasions:

> Therefore I urge you, imitate me. (1 Cor. 4:16)

> Imitate me, just as I also imitate Christ. (11:1)

> Brethren, join in following my example, and note those who so walk, as you have us for a pattern. (Phil. 3:17)

> And you became followers of us and of the Lord, having received the word in much affliction, with joy of the Holy Spirit. (1 Thess. 1:6)

> For you yourselves know how you ought to follow us, for we were not disorderly among you. (2 Thess. 3:7)

> Not because we do not have authority, but to make ourselves an example of how you should follow us. (3:9)

Paul obviously considered himself an example to the believers. In Philippians 4:9 he wrote, "The things which you learned and received and heard and saw in me, these do, and the God of peace will be with you."

When Timothy was just starting out in the ministry, Paul instructed him to be a model of the faith: "Let no one despise your youth, but be an example to the believers in word, in conduct, in love, in spirit, in faith, in purity" (1 Tim. 4:12).

Next to Christ, Paul stands out as the greatest example of a selfless lifestyle, and for many, his life is at a more reachable level than that of Christ:

> There are some who find Jesus Christ's very perfection daunting and rather discouraging. Because He inherited no sinful nature as we do, they feel that this fact conferred on Him a vast advantage, and removed Him from the arena of their earthly struggles and failures. He seems so far above them that they are able to draw very little practical help from His shining example. While this viewpoint springs from a misconception … its results are very real. In the apostle Paul God has provided the example of "a man just like us" (James 5:17). True, he was a man of towering spiritual stature, but he was also a man who knew failure along with his success…. Thus in Christ we find inspiration from a real Man who never failed, while in Paul we gain encouragement from a man who fell and rose again.[5]

HE WAS SELFLESS IN THE DISCIPLINE OF HIS OWN LIFE

When Paul wrote about being poured out on the sacrifice and service of faith, he was using an illustration that comes from the Old Testament—the drink offering. The regulations for the drink offering are not easy to discern, but we do know that this offering accompanied a larger sacrifice.

If you had watched the offering being presented, it would have looked something like this. The worshipper would bring his animal sacrifice to the altar and there would offer it unto the Lord. This sacrificial animal, having been killed and then totally consumed upon the altar, represented the total commitment of the Jewish worshipper. At this point the worshipper would make an additional offering called a libation. He would take a cup of wine and pour it upon the altar and the sacrifice that was already burning. Because the altar was hot, the libation would go up in a puff of smoke and be gone.

Paul was saying to the Philippians, "I know you are worried about my situation. I am in prison and could be executed at any moment. But my life is not the important thing. It is your faith that really counts. Your faith is the main offering. My life is just the drink offering that is poured out at the end." Paul viewed his own death as very unimportant when compared to the spiritual needs of the Philippian believers. He was filled with joy as he remembered his tireless labor on their behalf, because he placed the things of others above the things of his own life.

HE WAS SELFLESS IN DISCIPLING TIMOTHY

Another illustration of Paul's humble spirit is found in verse 22, where we read that Timothy served with him "as a son with his father." This paragraph reveals much about Timothy, but it also tells us a lot about Paul. We might expect the apostle to report that Timothy had served him as a son *to* a father. But instead he said that Timothy had served *with* him. They were coslaves. Paul shared his very life with Timothy, and there is no question that this was the secret to Timothy's progress and maturity. J. Oswald Sanders explains what this must have meant to the young disciple:

> Timothy would have been about twenty years of age when his tutelage began.... The record indicates that he needed more iron in his makeup. There was a tendency to be desultory about his work, and to be overtolerant and partial with important people.... He was apt to rely on an old spiritual experience instead of rekindling its dying flame. But Paul had very high and exacting aspirations for him, and did not spare him experiences or shelter him from hardships that would toughen his fiber and impart virility. He did not hesitate to assign to him tasks beyond his power. How else could a young man develop greater capacity than by tackling tasks which extended him to the utmost?

Traveling with Paul would bring Timothy into contact with men of all kinds, men of stature, whose personalities and achievements would kindle in him a wholesome ambition. From his tutor he learned how to meet triumphantly the crises which seemed routine in Paul's life and ministry.[6]

HE WAS SELFLESS IN DEALING WITH THE PHILIPPIANS

Paul saw his Christian friends as worthy of the best. He gave them Timothy, who, in Paul's estimation, had no equal. If ever there was a time when Paul needed Timothy, it was while he was under house arrest in Rome. He gave him up for the good of the Philippian believers. He gave them Epaphroditus, whom he loved and needed. In the phrase "service of your faith" (2:17), he used a word from which we get our word *liturgy*. He believed that service to others was a spiritual ministry. He was even prepared to give his life on behalf of the Philippians, if it came to that. As Christ had been obedient unto death so that Paul might have life, Paul was now willing to die, if need be, for those he loved. In fact, just before he was martyred, during his second Roman imprisonment, he wrote to Timothy, "I am now ready to be offered" (2 Tim. 4:6 KJV). This passage along with the reference here in Philippians 2 are the only two usages of this Greek expression in reference to human death. Paul was ready to be offered and he was indeed offered at last.

HE WAS SELFLESS IN DETERMINING GOD'S WILL

Paul was God's slave, and he functioned as a slave. His attitude toward sending Timothy to the Philippians was described as his *hope in the Lord* (see 2:23). His attitude toward returning to Philippi himself was *trust in the Lord* (2:24). In both instances, Paul cared only for the Lord's will.

What does it mean to be selfless as a Christian? Take a moment and ponder just two short verses from this Philippian letter. Someone has said that every Christian lives either in Philippians 1:21 or in Philippians 2:21. Look at these two verses side by side and ask yourself, "Which of these best describes my life?"

> Philippians 1:21—"For to me, to live is Christ, and to die is gain."

> Philippians 2:21—"For all seek their own, not the things which are of Christ Jesus."

Paul lived in Philippians 1:21. Jesus Christ was his life:

> He is a man without the care of making friends, without the hope or desire of worldly goods, without the apprehension of worldly loss, without the care of life, without the fear of death. He is a man of no rank, country or condition. A man of one thought—the Gospel of Christ. A man of

one purpose—the glory of Christ. A fool, and content to be reckoned a fool for Christ. Let him be called enthusiast, fanatic, babbler or any other outlandish nondescript the world may choose to denominate him. But still let him be nondescript. As soon as they call him trader, householder, citizen, man of wealth, man of the world, man of learning or even man of common sense, it is all over with his character. He must speak or he must die, and though he should die, he will speak. He has no rest but hastens over land and sea, over rocks and trackless deserts. He cries aloud and spares not, and will not be hindered. In the prisons he lifts up his voice, and in the tempests of the ocean, he is not silent. Before the awful councils and throned kings, he witnesses in behalf of the truth. Nothing can quench his voice but death, and even in the article of death, before the knife severed his head from his body, he speaks, he prays, he testifies, he confesses, he beseeches, he wars, and at length he blesses the cruel people.[7]

TIMOTHY: THE MODEL OF SERVICE

It is probable that Paul met Timothy on his first missionary journey (Acts 14:6). Timothy was probably converted at that time (1 Cor. 4:17). Paul considered Timothy his own dearly beloved son in the faith (2 Tim. 1:2). When Paul was on his second missionary journey, he enlisted Timothy to help him (Acts 16:1–4). Timothy is mentioned twenty-four times in Paul's letters and is identified with Paul in the writing of five letters. Here he is presented as a model of willing service to the Lord.

When Paul wrote of Timothy that he had no one "likeminded," he used a word that could literally be translated "of equal soul." Timothy was unique from those who put their own interests first. William Hendriksen put these words in Paul's mouth concerning Timothy:

> No one is better qualified and more favorably disposed. Already as a child he was an eager student of the sacred writings, a teachable and obedient son (2 Tim. 3:15). As he grew up he was highly recommended by those who knew him best (Acts 16:2). Upon his conversion to the Christian faith he became my beloved and faithful child in the Lord (1 Cor. 4:17), and a little later my special deputy and fellow worker (Rom. 16:21), always ready to go wherever I sent him or to be left behind wherever I told him to remain (Rom. 16:21). To top it all, he is God's minister in the Gospel of Christ (1 Thess. 3:2). And do not forget, either, that from the very founding of your church he has known you, and you have known him, not only was he present when your church

was established (Acts 16:11–40; 1 Thess. 2:2) but subsequently he has also visited you upon more than one occasion (Acts 19:21–22; 20:3–4; 2 Cor. 1:1). He therefore is a natural.[8]

IN HIS CONCERN FOR OTHERS, TIMOTHY SERVED

Paul described Timothy to the Philippians as one "who will sincerely care for your state" (Phil. 2:20). Timothy was naturally concerned for the welfare of the Philippians. His compassion was noteworthy because he was the only one to whom the apostle could point. The others were indifferent or were obsessed with their own agendas. Dwight Pentecost defines this problem as it occurs in our day:

> Here are saints to be taught. No one cares. Here are wounded hearts to be bound up. No one cares. Here are men to be reached for Christ. No one cares. Here are children to be taught and trained and guided in the things of the Lord, and no one cares.… Why? Too busy? Too preoccupied with their own business? No one cares.[9]

IN HIS CONSECRATION TO THE LORD, TIMOTHY SERVED

While all the others who had been chosen to serve with Paul put themselves first, Timothy was different. He was set apart from the rest because he put the things of Jesus Christ first (2:21). Timothy was not selfish; he was not in the ministry for what he could get out of it. He was a giver, not a taker. When Paul chose Timothy to accompany him on his missionary journeys, we are told that Timothy was "well spoken of by the brethren" (Acts 16:2).

IN HIS COMMITMENT TO THE GOSPEL, TIMOTHY SERVED

Timothy stood with Paul in the line of those who took the form of a slave. His whole life was given to the gospel. *Timothy's commitment to Jesus Christ was lived out in his commitment to others and to the gospel.*

In Philippians 2:20 we learn that Timothy was genuinely anxious for the welfare of the Philippian believers. In verse 21 we learn that he had as his ultimate goal the things of Jesus Christ. In verse 22 we learn that he was a servant of Paul for the gospel. *We seek the good of Christ by seeking the good of His people and of the gospel.*

EPAPHRODITUS: THE MODEL OF SUFFERING

Epaphroditus should not be confused with Epaphras, who was a member of the church at Colosse. Epaphroditus was a respected member of the church at Philippi. They had sent him to Rome to bring a gift to Paul and to stay with him as long as possible during his confinement. While Epaphroditus was in Rome he became seriously ill and almost died. He was miraculously restored to health, but not before the church in Philippi had experienced considerable anxiety on his behalf.

Paul decided to send Epaphroditus back to Philippi so they might see that he was in good health. He used the occasion to dispatch this letter to the church, instructing them to welcome Epaphroditus and acknowledge the sacrificial ministry he had extended to Paul.

Apart from these few verses, Epaphroditus would be an unknown, but in many respects, that fits him anyway. He was just a layman in the church at Philippi who held no office, wrote no books, gave no sermons, led no great enterprises for God. He was a messenger boy for the gospel, a servant for his Lord. No task was too menial for him to do. No assignment was too little for him to accept. No risk was too great for him to take. He would have been comfortable with a towel and basin.

Epaphroditus means "charming" or "lovely"; the name occurs only twice in the Bible, both times in this book. Besides this reference there is also mention of him in chapter 4, where Paul reported that he had received the gift from Epaphroditus that the Philippians had sent (v. 18).

Paul loved Epaphroditus and identified closely with him. They were united in "common sympathy, common work, and common danger."[10]

When he called him a "*brother*," Paul selected one of his favorite terms for fellow Christians. He used the word nine times in this short letter (1:12, 14; 2:25; 3:1, 13, 17; 4:1, 8, 21). Paul and Epaphroditus were united as brothers in the same spiritual family.

But Paul went beyond this family relationship to describe Ephaphroditus as a "*fellow worker*." This is another favorite Pauline characterization, and he used it elsewhere to describe Apollos, Aquila and Priscilla, Aristarchus, Clement, Mark, Onesimus, Philemon, Timothy, and Titus.

Finally, Epaphroditus is described as a *"fellow soldier."* It is never enough to be just a worker in the ministry. One must also learn to be a warrior. The enemies and foes are multiplied as the ministry increases. Paul was the first to see the open doors of opportunity, but he also recognized that "there are many adversaries" (1 Cor. 16:9). Apparently Epaphroditus had learned how to put on the whole armor of God and to stand against the strategies of the Devil. He, like Paul, knew that the war was not with flesh and blood but with principalities and powers and rulers of darkness and spiritual wickedness in high places (Eph. 6:11–12).

These three descriptions of Epaphroditus point to a man who had a cooperative spirit. He was not just a worker or a soldier; he was a *fellow worker* and a *fellow soldier* and a *brother*.

IN HIS SERVICE TO PAUL, EPAPHRODITUS SUFFERED

To the Philippians, Paul described Epaphroditus as "your messenger and the one who ministered to my need" (2:25). Twice we are told that Epaphroditus risked his life in order to minister to Paul (vv. 27, 30). The phrase "not regarding his life" is a translation of the Greek word *paraboleumai*, and this is the only time it is used in the New Testament. In the language of the common people it meant "to gamble or bet." In other words, Epaphroditus gambled his very life to fulfill the work he had been given to do. He gambled his life to come to Rome in search of Paul. The early Christians called those who risked their lives for Christ "Parabolani" or "the Riskers." Aquila and Priscilla would have been members of that group. Paul wrote of them in Romans, "Greet Priscilla and Aquila, my fellow workers in Christ Jesus, who risked their own necks for my life" (16:3–4). John the apostle told of other heroes of faith who "did not love their lives to the death" (Rev. 12:11).

The phrase "God had mercy on him" is very interesting because it implies that, though the health of Epaphroditus was deteriorating, Paul was no longer performing miracles of healing to authenticate his apostleship. There is no indication that Paul laid hands on Epaphroditus and conferred healing on him. Dr. H. A. Ironside observes:

> Let it be noted that the apostle did not consider he had any right to demand physical healing even for so faithful a laborer as Epaphroditus. Paul recognized it as simply the mercy of God, not as that to which saints have a right. This is true divine healing. And let it be remembered that sickness may be as really from God as health. It is clear that Paul never held or taught "healing in the atonement" and therefore the birthright privilege of all Christians. Nor do we ever read of him or his fellow-laborers being miraculously healed. Paul himself, Trophimus, Timothy and Epaphroditus, all bear witness to the contrary.[11]

EPAPHRODITUS SUFFERED

When Epaphroditus heard that the Philippians were worrying about him he was "full of heaviness" (v. 26 KJV). This is the expression that describes our Lord's troubled spirit in the garden of Gethsemane. It is a very strong word of emotion. Far from being glad that he was the center of attention back home, Epaphroditus was sick with concern that they were worrying about him. So Paul sent him back to Philippi and asked the Philippians not only to receive him but to honor him.

As I think about Paul, Timothy, and Epaphroditus, I am challenged in my own life. While it may seem to us, at times, that the Christian life is beyond our reach, these flesh-and-blood examples spur us on to a new level of allegiance to our Savior. If I had to sum up the character of these heroes of the faith, I could do no better than to echo the words of Bishop Ryle:

> A zealous man in religion is preeminently a man of one thing.... He sees only one thing, he cares for one thing, he lives for one thing, he is swallowed up for one thing; and that one thing is to please God. Whether he lives, or whether he dies, whether he has health, or whether he has sickness, whether he is rich, or whether he is poor, whether he pleases man, or whether he gives offense, whether he is thought wise, or whether he is thought foolish, whether he gets honor, or whether he gets shame, for all this the ... man

cares nothing at all. He burns for one thing; and that one thing is to please God and to advance God's glory.[12]

David Michell, the little boy who was imprisoned with Eric Liddell, saw the same quality in his hero. He wrote:

What was his secret? He unreservedly committed his life to Jesus Christ as his Saviour and Lord. That friendship meant everything to him. By the flickering light of a peanut-oil lamp, early each morning he and a room-mate in the men's cramped dormitory studied the Bible and talked with God for an hour. As a Christian, Eric Liddell's desire was to know God more deeply, and as a missionary, to make him known more fully.[13]

Finally, my brethren, rejoice in the Lord.
For me to write the same things to you
is not tedious, but for you it is safe.

Beware of dogs, beware of evil workers, beware
of the mutilation! For we are the circumcision,
who worship God in the Spirit, rejoice in Christ
Jesus, and have no confidence in the flesh, though
I also might have confidence in the flesh. If anyone
else thinks he may have confidence in the flesh, I
more so: circumcised the eighth day, of the stock
of Israel, of the tribe of Benjamin, a Hebrew of
the Hebrews; concerning the law, a Pharisee;
concerning zeal, persecuting the church; concerning
the righteousness which is in the law, blameless.

Philippians 3:1–6

THE JOY OF HUMILITY

Philippians 3:1–6

Rejoice in Christ Jesus, and have no confidence in the flesh.

In 1858, a small, frail lad was born to a rich family in New York. Along with feeble eyesight, he suffered from asthma so severe that he sometimes couldn't blow out the bedside candle; nevertheless, he became one of the most powerful men on earth. At eleven years of age, his father told him that a good mind alone would not ensure success, that he must build himself a powerful new body to match it. So the lad spent thousands of hours chinning himself, lifting weights, and rattling a punching bag.

It is little wonder that he rose like a rocket in the world of politics. He was elected to the New York legislature at twenty-three; was a candidate for mayor at twenty-eight; was US Civil Service commissioner under two presidents; president of the Police Commission of New York; national hero as leader of the Rough

Riders in the Spanish-American War at forty; then, in just three busy years, governor of New York, vice president, and finally president of the United States of America. In 1905, Teddy Roosevelt received the Nobel Peace Prize for his efforts in helping to end the Russo-Japanese War. At five feet nine inches, Roosevelt was a small man who was made large through his commitment.[1]

In many respects, the early life of Teddy Roosevelt parallels that of the apostle Paul. They both inherited advantages and they both worked hard to give themselves additional advantages. There is one huge difference, however, that becomes evident in the section of Scripture we are about to study. Roosevelt climbed to success in the system of the world. Paul became a success in the plan of God. All the things Roosevelt accomplished were stepping-stones for his ultimate achievement. All the things Paul accomplished (Phil. 3:5–6) were stumbling blocks to his acceptance with God. In comparing these two men we are reminded of the words of our Lord recorded by the prophet Isaiah:

> "For My thoughts are not your thoughts,
> Nor are your ways My ways," says the LORD.
> "For as the heavens are higher than the earth,
> So are My ways higher than your ways,
> And My thoughts than your thoughts." (55:8–9)

The verses we are looking at in this section were the result of Paul's deep love for his friends at Philippi, who were being asked to mix the grace of God with the works of the flesh. Sinister teachers of legalism had crept into the body, attempting to seduce the Philippians into adding circumcision to the plan of salvation. Paul warned against these intruders and then explained that their premise was unsound. For if anyone could be recommended to God by virtue of accomplishment, Paul argued that he would be that person! If Paul had failed to achieve acceptance with God through all his inherited and earned virtues, then, he reasoned, no one could climb up to God on his own merits.

THE APOSTLE'S SERIOUS WARNING

The opening command sets the tone for the entire chapter—"rejoice in the Lord." The Philippians were not to rejoice in who they were and what they had done. They were to rejoice in Jesus Christ and all that He had done.

Paul acknowledged that he was repeating a warning he had already given them, but he said, "To write the same things to you is not tedious." All the things Paul was about to say had been said before in this letter. He had already spoken of unity, of adversaries, of standing firm, of being in one spirit, and of holding forth God's Word as a light to a dark generation. Yet he would repeat his admonitions because he loved these brethren in Philippi and cared about their spiritual safety.

Paul's concern for the Philippians was no different than the uneasiness he expressed when he was bidding farewell to the Ephesian elders:

> For I know this, that after my departure savage wolves will come in among you, not sparing the

flock. Also from among yourselves men will rise up, speaking perverse things, to draw away the disciples after themselves. Therefore watch, and remember that for three years I did not cease to warn everyone night and day with tears. (Acts 20:29–31)

Paul was neither angry nor bitter, but he was bold and blunt. Earlier he had demonstrated a spirit of tolerance toward those who were preaching the gospel from wrong motives. But there was no tolerance here for the Judaizers who were telling the believers that they must become Jews before they could become Christians.

They were actually teaching that a man had to be circumcised after the manner of Moses or he could not be a part of God's family. We read of such an invasion of the gospel of grace in Acts 15:1. "And certain men came down from Judea and taught the brethren, 'Unless you are circumcised according to the custom of Moses, you cannot be saved.'"

This perversion of the gospel had Paul exercised in his spirit, and he used the term *beware* three times. He branded these false teachers as "dogs," "evil workers," and "mutilation." He was not making reference here to three different brands of false teachers but was describing the Judaizers in three different ways.

BEWARE OF DOGS

This uncomplimentary term is found in numerous passages in both the Old and New Testaments.

As a dog returns to his own vomit, so a fool repeats his folly. (Prov. 26:11)

But it has happened to them according to the true proverb: "A dog returns to his own vomit," and, "a sow, having washed, to her wallowing in the mire." (2 Pet. 2:22)

Awake to punish all the nations; do not be merciful to any wicked transgressors. Selah. At evening they return, they growl like a dog, and go all around the city. (Ps. 59:5–6)

But outside are dogs and sorcerers and sexually immoral and murderers and idolaters, and whoever loves and practices a lie. (Rev. 22:15)

But [Jesus] answered and said, "It is not good to take the children's bread and throw it to the little dogs." (Matt. 15:26)

The term *dogs* in Philippians describes the false teachers who were bringing legalism into the Christian gospel. They were like the false prophets of Isaiah's day:

His watchmen are blind, they are all ignorant; they are all dumb dogs, they cannot bark; sleeping, lying

COUNT IT ALL JOY

down, loving to slumber. Yes, they are greedy dogs
which never have enough. And they are shepherds
who cannot understand; they all look to their own
way, every one for his own gain, from his own
territory. (56:10–11)

BEWARE OF EVIL WORKERS

The "evil workers" were those who wormed their way into the
congregation and taught a form of teaching other than the gospel.
They were aggressive in disseminating their works-salvation; they
were working for their own redemption and teaching that it must
be so for everyone. They believed that their zeal in influencing
others to follow them was a part of their being accepted by God.
They were like the Pharisees who traveled anywhere to make just
one convert (Matt. 23:15).

In writing to the Corinthians, Paul called these same intruders
"false apostles, deceitful workers, transforming themselves into
apostles of Christ" (2 Cor. 11:13). F. B. Meyer described the modern version of such teachers:

> They are not set upon doing all the harm they
> can in the world, but are fanatical, unbalanced,
> and unable to distinguish between a part and the
> whole, magnifying some microscopical point in
> Christianity until it blinds the eye to the symme-
> try, proportion, and beauty of Heaven's glorious
> scheme. These people are the "cranks" of our

churches; they introduce fads and hobbies; they exaggerate the importance of trifles; they catch up every new theory and vagary, and follow it to the detriment of truth and love. It is impossible to exaggerate the harm that these people do.[2]

BEWARE OF THE MUTILATION

The word *mutilation* refers to the cutting of circumcision. When these false teachers were requiring the believers to be circumcised in order to be saved, they were mutilating the flesh of these brothers. The gospel of grace preached by Paul declared that salvation came through Jesus Christ and not through the works of the flesh. If, then, the gospel was complete in the realm of faith, anything that would be added to that would be as nothing with God. In other words, all the cutting involved for the rite of circumcision was nothing more than meaningless mutilation of the flesh.

Someone has observed that these teachers invited men to Christ with the Scriptures in one hand and a knife in the other. Paul condemned them in his letter to the Galatians:

> As many as desire to make a good showing in the flesh, these would compel you to be circumcised, only that they may not suffer persecution for the cross of Christ. For not even those who are circumcised keep the law, but they desire to have you circumcised that they may boast in your flesh. (6:12–13)

This problem that Paul so ruthlessly attacked as Judaism is still with us today in the church. We usually refer to it as legalism.

> One of the most serious problems facing the orthodox Christian church today is the problem of legalism. One of the most serious problems facing the church in Paul's day was the problem of legalism. In every day it is the same. Legalism wrenches the joy of the Lord from the Christian believer, and with the joy of the Lord goes his power for vital worship and vibrant service. Nothing is left but cramped, somber, dull, and listless profession. The truth is betrayed, and the glorious name of the Lord becomes a synonym for a gloomy kill-joy. The Christian under the law is a miserable parody of the real thing.[3]

Tim Hansel describes a modern legalist in a way that helps us understand why Paul was so vehement in his denunciation of these Judaizing teachers who were trying to contaminate the Philippians:

> Irony of ironies, his commitment to Jesus Christ has become a prison rather than a blessing. So blinded by religious observations and reservations, he fails to see the festivity that was

so central in the life of Jesus. He forgets that Jesus, despite the sad world he inhabited, was the prime host and the prime guest of the party. Jesus let himself be doused with perfume. He attended to wedding wine and wedding garments. The Bible is full of merriment. The feast outruns the fast.[4]

THE APOSTLE'S SPIRITUAL WORSHIP

In contrast to all that was being recommended by the Judaizers, Paul went on to describe the true worshipper.

THE TRUE WORSHIPPER RESPONDS TO GOD IN THE SPIRIT

Jesus taught, "God is Spirit, and those who worship Him must worship in spirit and truth" (John 4:24). True believers worship in the power of the Holy Spirit, and that worship takes place in their human spirit.

THE TRUE WORSHIPPER REJOICES IN CHRIST JESUS ALONE

Paul taught that every true believer finds his joy not in the cutting of the flesh but in the person of Jesus Christ. In writing to the Galatians, Paul said, "But God forbid that I should boast except in the cross of our Lord Jesus Christ, by whom the world has been crucified to me, and I to the world" (6:14).

THE TRUE WORSHIPPER REFUSES TO TRUST IN THE FLESH

Paul's threefold description concluded with a reaffirmation that the believer has "no confidence in the flesh." A true believer knows he is not capable of earning God's favor through the deeds or works of the flesh. In the story Jesus told of the two men who came to pray, the one who recommended himself to the Lord on the basis of all he had done was rejected. The one who cried, "God, be merciful to me a sinner!" was received (Luke 18:9–14).

THE APOSTLE'S SEVEN ASSETS

If anyone had a legitimate right to justify himself before God, Paul was certainly that man. On the basis of his inherited privileges and earnest endeavors, he would qualify, if anyone could. He said seven things about himself.

CIRCUMCISED THE EIGHTH DAY

When circumcision was given by God as the sign of His covenant with Abraham, Abraham was ninety-nine years old and Ishmael was thirteen (Gen. 17:1–14, 24–25). From that day on, every Jewish male was to be circumcised on the eighth day after his birth (17:12; Lev. 12:3). Jesus was circumcised on the eighth day (Luke 2:21). Only those who became converts to Judaism were circumcised as adults. This was at the top of Paul's list because the Judaizers were demanding this of the Philippians. Paul went right to the heart of their argument. He knew many of the false teachers had not been circumcised themselves, since they were converts to Judaism as adults.

OF THE STOCK OF ISRAEL

Paul's roots were traceable back to the patriarchs. He was not a convert to Judaism but had been a Jew from his birth. On both sides, his genealogy was pure. In his second letter to the Corinthians, he affirmed his Jewishness: "Are they Hebrews? So am I. Are they Israelites? So am I. Are they the seed of Abraham? So am I" (11:22).

OF THE TRIBE OF BENJAMIN

Benjamin was the last of the twelve sons born to Jacob. Out of the tribe of Benjamin came Israel's first king, Saul. Some believe that Paul's parents named him Saul after King Saul. The Benjamites were the aristocracy of Israel. To be a Benjamite was to be truly an Israelite!

HEBREW OF THE HEBREWS

This simply meant that Paul was a Hebrew boy born to Hebrew parents. He spoke the Hebrew language and lived by the Hebrew customs. He was schooled in the Hebrew tradition under a very honored teacher named Gamaliel. In one of his sermons, Paul told of his background:

> I am indeed a Jew, born in Tarsus of Cilicia, but
> brought up in this city at the feet of Gamaliel,
> taught according to the strictness of our fathers'

law, and was zealous toward God as you all are today. (Acts 22:3)

The providence of God was certainly at work in Paul's life when he was given the opportunity to sit under the teaching of Gamaliel.

> Gamaliel was called "the beauty of the law." This learned and notable rabbi was one of seven Jewish doctors of the law to whom was given the honored title of "Rabban." He was of the school of Hillel, which embraced a broader and more liberal view than that of Shammai. Paul was thus exposed to a wider spectrum of teaching than would otherwise have been the case. Unlike Shammai, Gamaliel was interested in Greek literature and encouraged Jews to have friendship and social intercourse with foreigners. From him, young Saul probably learned sincerity and honesty of judgment, as well as a willingness to study and use the works of Gentile authors.[5]

Paul's pride of ancestry is summarized, then, in these four statements: he was circumcised the eighth day, of the stock of Israel, of the tribe of Benjamin, and a Hebrew of the Hebrews. He could boast in his ancestry, but he could also boast in his orthodoxy.

A PHARISEE

Paul claimed to be not only a Jew but also a Pharisee among the Jews. Even after his three missionary journeys, he still claimed that association. "I am a Pharisee, the son of a Pharisee" (Acts 23:6). The Pharisees were the strictest and most conservative of the Jewish sects. When Paul stood before King Agrippa, he described himself this way:

> My manner of life from my youth, which was spent from the beginning among my own nation at Jerusalem, all the Jews know. They knew me from the first, if they were willing to testify, that according to the strictest sect of our religion I lived a Pharisee. (26:4–5)

Not only did Paul consider himself to be a Pharisee, but he also boasted in the fact that he was the strictest of the Pharisees: "And I advanced in Judaism beyond many of my contemporaries in my own nation, being more exceedingly zealous for the traditions of my fathers" (Gal. 1:14).

For Paul, being a Pharisee was not the negative experience that we normally read into that term today:

> In our day the word Pharisee is a synonym for religious pride and hypocrisy; but we must never forget that in those old Jewish days the Pharisee represented some of the noblest

traditions of the Hebrew people. Amid the prevailing indifference the Pharisees stood for a strict religious life. As against the skepticism of the Sadducees, who believed in neither spirit nor unseen world, the Pharisees held to the resurrection of the dead, and the life of the world to come. Amid the lax morals of the time, which infected Jerusalem almost as much as Rome, the Pharisee was austere in his ideals, and holy in life.[6]

Remember that Paul's purpose in citing all this biographical information was simply to prove that if anyone had the right to boast in the flesh, he certainly did. The Judaizers who were trying to indoctrinate the Philippians claimed righteousness by means of self-effort, but they did not even measure up to Paul.

A ZEALOUS PERSECUTOR OF THE CHURCH

We are not left to wonder about Paul's religious zeal, for he points to his fanatical activity as a Pharisee. Before he met the Lord on the Damascus road, he was as committed to persecuting the Christians as he later was to teaching them. The word *persecute* is in the present tense, which leads us to believe that Paul's persecution of the Christians was not a once in a while activity but rather a lifetime pledge. As a strict Pharisee, he believed that killing Christians was a noble service to God. According to his own statement, he took his gruesome assignment seriously:

> I persecuted this Way to the death, binding and delivering into prisons both men and women, as also the high priest bears me witness, and all the council of the elders, from whom I also received letters to the brethren, and went to Damascus to bring in chains even those who were there to Jerusalem to be punished. (Acts 22:4–5)

> Many of the saints I shut up in prison, having received authority from the chief priests; and when they were put to death, I cast my vote against them. And I punished them often in every synagogue and compelled them to blaspheme; and being exceedingly enraged against them, I persecuted them even to foreign cities. (26:10–11)

When Stephen was martyred, Paul consented to his death (Acts 8:1). Later on he would say, "And when the blood of Your martyr Stephen was shed, I also was standing by consenting to his death, and guarding the clothes of those who were killing him" (22:20).

Even after his conversion, Paul was feared by the believers because of his reputation: "And when Saul had come to Jerusalem, he tried to join the disciples; but they were all afraid of him, and did not believe that he was a disciple" (9:26).

BLAMELESS BEFORE THE LAW

Next we are told that Paul was blameless under the law. This certainly did not mean he was sinless. It simply meant he kept the outward rules of the law so meticulously that no one could point an accusing finger at him. There was nothing to bring against the name or religion of Paul.

> He would hold it a crime to enter into the house of a Gentile; and on leaving market or street he would carefully wash his hands of any defilement contracted through touching what had been handled by the uncircumcised.... He was taught to fast twice in the week, and give tithes of all he possessed. He would observe the Sabbath and festivals with punctilious and awful care.[7]

Yes, if there was anyone who had the right to boast in the flesh, it was Paul. He had the right ancestry, he was orthodox in his religion, his activity backed up his belief system, and his own outward lifestyle was without blame. If anyone could be recommended to God on the basis of his self-merit, Paul qualified. But that was just the point he wished to make. He was not acceptable to God because of his background or religious acts. Before he could come to God, he had to turn his back on all these things and trust only in Christ.

George Whitefield was one of the most effective preachers of the gospel the church has ever known. His preaching trips to

America were largely responsible for the Great Awakening that took place in the middle of the eighteenth century. As a teenager, Whitefield had desired to live a religious and serious life. When he enrolled in college, he began to pray and sing psalms three times every day, in addition to his regular morning and evening devotional time. He religiously fasted every Friday and always on that day received the sacrament of Communion at a parish church near his college. He habitually attended public worship and abstained from worldly pleasures. But during all this time, just like Paul, George Whitefield was lost.

One day he was introduced to Charles Wesley, who gave Whitefield a copy of a book by Henry Scougal, *The Life of God in the Soul of Man*. When George Whitefield read that book he realized he was not saved. In one of his sermons, he recalled what happened:

> I must bear testimony to my old friend Mr. Charles Wesley. He put a book into my hands ... whereby God showed me that I must be born again or be damned.... I learned that a man may go to church, say his prayers, receive the Sacrament, and yet not be a Christian. How did my heart rise and shudder like a poor man that is afraid to look into his ledger lest he should find himself bankrupt....
>
> "Shall I burn this book? Shall I throw it down? or shall I search it?" I did search it: and,

holding the book in my hand, thus addressed the God of heaven and earth: "Lord if I am not a Christian, for Jesus Christ's sake show me what Christianity is, that I may not be damned at last." I read a little further, and discovered that they who know anything of religion know it is a vital union with the Son of God—Christ formed in the heart. O what a ray of divine life did then break in upon my soul![8]

For Paul, just as for George Whitefield, there could be no salvation until all objects of faith were removed and Christ alone was at the center of his heart!

But what things were gain to me, these I have counted loss for Christ. Yet indeed I also count all things loss for the excellence of the knowledge of Christ Jesus my Lord, for whom I have suffered the loss of all things, and count them as rubbish, that I may gain Christ and be found in Him, not having my own righteousness, which is from the law, but that which is through faith in Christ, the righteousness which is from God by faith; that I may know Him and the power of His resurrection, and the fellowship of His sufferings, being conformed to His death, if, by any means, I may attain to the resurrection from the dead.

Not that I have already attained, or am already perfected; but I press on, that I may lay hold of that for which Christ Jesus has also laid hold of me. Brethren, I do not count myself to have apprehended; but one thing I do, forgetting those things which are behind and reaching forward to those things which are ahead, I press toward the goal for the prize of the upward call of God in Christ Jesus.

Philippians 3:7–14

8

THE JOY OF VICTORY

Philippians 3:7–14

What things were gain to me, these I have counted loss for Christ.

Before he died, Vince Lombardi, the legendary coach of the Green Bay Packers, put into writing the philosophy to which he attributed his great success. The brief statement titled "What It Takes to Be Number One" is hanging on locker room walls wherever the game of football is played. Here, in part, is what Lombardi said:

> You've got to pay the price. Winning is not a some-time thing; it's an all-the-time thing. You don't win once in a while; you don't do things right once in a while; you do them right all the time. Winning is a habit. Unfortunately, so is losing....
>
> Every time a football player goes out to ply his trade, he's got to play from the ground

up—from the soles of his feet right up to his head. Every inch of him has to play. Some guys play with their heads. That's O.K. You've got to be smart to be number one in any business. But more important, you've got to play with your heart—with every fiber of your body. If you … find a guy with a lot of head and a lot of heart, he's never going to come off the field second.[1]

Few men live with such passionate commitment! Vince Lombardi poured his heart and soul into the challenge of championship football.

Another champion of an earlier day also left his philosophy of winning behind, and we have it before us in the third chapter of Philippians. In a clear and motivating statement, Paul tells us what it takes to win, to reach the goal, to achieve. For him and for us the goal is far more compelling. It calls us to be winners in our relationship with the Lord Jesus Christ.

As Paul looked over his shoulder at his past, he made an honest evaluation. As he looked forward to his future, he charted out some lofty goals. Most of all he set out a strategy that had immediate impact on his lifestyle. His message is strong! His challenge needs to be prominently displayed in the locker room of our souls.

THE LIABILITIES OF THE PAST

Saul was on his way to Damascus to persecute the Christians when the life-changing event took place. All his values were reversed. The things that had been important to him were no longer of any consequence. The things that had been gain to him he now counted as loss. Before he met the Lord, Paul measured the success of his life by his physical ancestry, his religious orthodoxy, his spiritual activity, and his personal morality. But when the Savior laid hold of him, all this was altered. The things he had never cared about now became the objects of his greatest concern.

> The bitterest foe became the greatest friend. The blasphemer became the preacher of Christ's love. The hand that wrote the indictment of the disciples of Christ when he brought them before the magistrates and into prison now penned epistles of God's redeeming love. The heart that once beat with joy when Stephen sank beneath the bloody stones now rejoiced in scourgings and stonings for the sake of Christ. From this erstwhile enemy, persecutor, blasphemer came the greater part of the New Testament, the noblest statements of theology, the sweetest lyrics of Christian love.[2]

As Paul evaluated his former life, he used the plural of the word *gain* to describe his evaluation. He listed all his assets item by item, one by one, and as he totaled them up, he discovered they had all moved from the *asset* column to the *liability* column, adding up to a gigantic zero. Dr. H. A. Ironside wrote:

He was not simply exchanging one religion for another; it was not one system of rites and ceremonies giving place to a superior system; or one set of doctrines, rules and regulations making way for a better one.... He had come in contact with a divine Person, the once crucified, but now glorified Christ of God. He had been won by that Person forever, and for His sake he counted all else but loss.... Christ, and Christ alone, meets every need of the soul.[3]

The word Paul used to describe this deficit total was *loss* or *zemian*. Outside of this epistle, it is used only in Acts 27, where it describes the loss and damage suffered by the ship on which Paul was taken as a prisoner to Rome (vv. 10, 21). The story pictures how that which is gain can become loss. The ship headed for Italy had cargo aboard that was meant to bring gain to its owner. If the crew had not thrown the wheat overboard, all the passengers on board could have been casualties. The cargo was thrown overboard and the ship broken up, but the passengers and crew were saved (vv. 38–41).

Everything that was to be gain became loss so that the passengers might be saved. For the apostle, all the "cargo" of his past life had to be thrown overboard so that he might gain his own spiritual life in Christ.

That is an experience many have known. Born into Christian homes, children of spiritual leaders, members of good churches, they, like Paul, had to discount their privileges as a means of having Christ. To some, this may not seem like a strange requirement, but the Lord's words put it into perspective:

> For whoever desires to save his life will lose it, but whoever loses his life for My sake will find it. For what profit is it to a man if he gains the whole world, and loses his own soul? Or what will a man give in exchange for his soul? (Matt. 16:25–26)

In Philippians 3:7–8, Paul used the word *count* three times. In this context, the word *count* means "to evaluate or to consider." Paul was reminding the Philippians that the decision he made some thirty years before still had its hold on him. He had not changed his mind! He still counted his previous assets as liabilities.

Paul went a step further, for he counted not only the seven things listed in verses 5 and 6 as useless in winning Christ, but he put "all things" in that same category. Nothing but the righteousness that is in Christ remained on the asset side of Paul's balance sheet.

He used a graphic word to describe his previous attempts to merit favor with God. He called them "rubbish." There are two possible meanings of this word. It could mean bodily excrement, or it might also refer to the food leftovers that were thrown to the dogs. Both possibilities define "useless waste."

The values that the legalists placed as priorities on their lists, Paul called refuse. Back in verse 2, the apostle had referred to these legalists as dogs. He now identified their values as worthless trash, food for dogs. The credibility of the apostle's evaluation is this: not only did he *count* the loss of all things, but he actually *suffered* the loss of all things.

THE POSSIBILITIES OF THE FUTURE

When Paul said he wanted to "gain Christ," he used the same Greek word for "gain" in verse 7. Paul had turned away from the gain of his former life in order to obtain the gain of Christ. He was not talking about gaining Christ as his Savior. That had happened thirty years before. Rather, he was expressing his deep desire to know Christ better and to develop Christlikeness in his own life.

In Philippians 2, we read that Jesus Christ was found in human form. Because He was found in human form, anyone who saw Him thought Him to be a man. Paul's expressed desire was exactly that! He prayed that as he was found in Christ, anyone who saw him would consider him as one who belonged to Christ.

In order to comprehend Paul's statement about not having his own righteousness, we need to remember that he had been carefully contrasting two different kinds of righteousness. There was first of all "my own righteousness," and second, "the righteousness which is from God by faith." He had learned by experience that God's righteousness had changed him in a way his own righteousness could never do. Instead of being just outwardly righteous, Paul now had a righteous heart. He understood that the labors of his hands could never fulfill the law's demands. "For the LORD does not see as man sees; for man looks at the outward appearance, but the LORD looks at the heart" (1 Sam. 16:7).

KNOWING THE PERSON OF CHRIST

One of Paul's continuing goals was to know the Lord Jesus Christ. The word *know* means to know by experience. It is more than just being acquainted with someone. It is possible to know a person casually and not know him personally. We all know the president of the United States; that is, we know who he is. But very few of us know him personally. Former Los Angeles Dodgers pitcher Orel Hershiser tells about the time when Frank Sinatra gave him and his wife, Jamie, an autographed photo: "He signed it, 'To my great friends,' and he spelled our names 'Oral and Jane.' Goes to show you how good of friends we really were."[4]

Many who consider themselves Christians have a knowledge of Christ that is not experiential but intellectual. The knowledge Paul is talking about here goes deeper. It is the surpassing knowledge of Jesus Christ that he already mentioned in Philippians 3:8.

This is our Lord's desire for us, as expressed in His prayer: "And this is eternal life, that they may know You, the only true God, and Jesus Christ whom You have sent" (John 17:3).

This is the prayer Paul prayed for the Ephesian believers: "That you may know … what is the exceeding greatness of His power toward us who believe, according to the working of His mighty power which He worked in Christ when He raised Him from the dead" (1:18–20). Paul's desire for the Ephesians ought to be the focus of every believer. We should have as our goal to "grow in the grace and knowledge of our Lord and Savior Jesus Christ" (2 Pet. 3:18). This knowledge of the person of Jesus Christ is what sets Christianity apart from all the religions of the world. Our faith is not one of systems and doctrines and regulations and rituals. Our faith is personal and intimate. We know a Person who has changed our lives and we live in fellowship with Him. He lives within us by His Spirit, and we can know Him better and better as we walk with Him day by day.

"But," you may ask, "if I already know Him as my Savior, how do I come to know Him better? If I desire to be completely wrapped up in Christ, how do I go about it?" Here is a concise answer to that question from the pen of William Hendriksen:

> One gains such experiential knowledge by wide-awake attendance at public worship and proper use of the sacraments, by showing kindness to all, practicing the forgiving spirit, above all love; by learning to be thankful; by studying the Word of Christ both devotionally and exegetically so that it dwells in the heart; by singing psalms, hymns, and spiritual songs to the glory of God, and continuing steadfastly in prayer; and thus by redeeming the time as a witness of Christ to all men.[5]

KNOWING THE POWER OF CHRIST

In his letter to the Ephesians, Paul spoke of God's "mighty power which He worked in Christ when He raised Him from the dead." And then he told those believers that the exceeding greatness of this power comes to us who believe (1:18–20).

As believers, we have known the power of Christ's resurrection in the *past*, because at the moment of our conversion, we were raised up with Christ and seated in heavenly places (2:6). We can know that power in the *present*, for Christ's resurrection was accomplished so that we might "walk in newness of life" (Rom. 6:4). We will know that power completely in the *future* when our bodies will be raised up just as His was (1 Cor. 15).

It is interesting to observe that Paul used a reverse order to list the events of Christ's life that correspond to us. It is resurrection first, death second, and suffering third. Spiritual resurrection is the beginning place for us all. We were dead in sin but we have been raised to new life in Christ. Each day as we grow spiritually, we are being conformed to His death. Just as the caterpillar is formed invisibly so that it might emerge as a butterfly, so we are being conformed to His death day by day. Of course, a large part of that process of conformation is suffering.

KNOWING THE PASSION OF CHRIST

When Paul was converted, the Lord spoke to Ananias about Paul's future suffering: "For I will show him how many things he must suffer for My name's sake" (Acts 9:16). Now the imprisoned apostle actually prayed for the opportunity of identifying with Christ in His passion. The sufferings that Paul desired to know were not those of Christ's crucifixion, or even of his own martyrdom, but the suffering that is experienced by the believer who is totally committed to Jesus Christ. He spoke of it earlier when he said that for the sake of Christ he had suffered the loss of all things (Phil. 3:8).

Peter wrote of this suffering to his readers, "For to this you were called, because Christ also suffered for us, leaving us an example, that you should follow His steps" (1 Pet. 2:21). He described this as suffering for doing good (2:20), suffering for righteousness' sake (3:14), suffering for the name of Christ (4:14), suffering as a Christian (4:16), and suffering according to the will of God (4:19). Jesus considered such suffering a blessing:

> Blessed are those who are persecuted for righteousness' sake, for theirs is the kingdom of heaven. Blessed are you when they revile and persecute you, and say all kinds of evil against you falsely for My sake. Rejoice and be exceedingly glad, for great is your reward in heaven, for so they persecuted the prophets who were before you. (Matt. 5:10–12)

Robert Laidlaw, author of the famous tract "The Reason Why," said that in his many travels around the world he had seen many mottos with the words "Saved to Serve" but that he had never seen a motto with the words "Saved to Suffer." But here Paul was expressing his desire to fellowship with the Lord in His sufferings. Phillips translated this phrase, "I long to share his sufferings" (Phil. 3:11).

Earlier in this letter, Paul had written this to the Philippians: "For to you it has been granted on behalf of Christ, not only to believe in Him, but also to suffer for His sake" (1:29). The lesson is clear: if we are to share in the glories of Christ, we must also share in His sufferings. "If indeed we suffer with Him, that we may also be glorified together" (Rom. 8:17).

KNOWING THE PRAISE OF CHRIST

Philippians 3:11 is the only place in the New Testament where this form of the Greek word for "resurrection" is used. Literally it means "out-resurrection," the resurrection "out from the dead ones." When the dead in Christ shall rise at the time of the rapture, the next event is the rewarding of the saints at the judgment seat of Christ. Paul was speaking of that moment when he would stand before the Lord; he did not want to be empty-handed. Whatever he would attain in that day, he would have to earn in this life as he strived to please his Master (Matt. 24:44–47; 1 John 2:28).

THE RESPONSIBILITIES OF THE PRESENT

If Paul wanted to know the person of his Lord more intimately and the power of his Lord more fully, if he dared to enter into the suffering of his Lord more completely, and if he hoped to stand before his Lord someday and hear the words "Well done, thou good and faithful servant!"—if all of these were to be true, then what was his present responsibility?

Here is a powerful prescription for believers everywhere. If you want to know joy in the future, here is what you must do today.

DEVELOP THE DISCIPLINE TO FOCUS

In the athletic world, the name of the game is concentration! If an athlete cannot concentrate, if he cannot teach himself to focus, he will not be able to compete. Players talk of being in a "zone," where their concentration is so intense that it blocks out the rest of the world. They do not hear the crowd noises. They do not feel the pain of injury. They are focused!

This same kind of concentration is a requirement for those who would "gain Christ." Nothing must be allowed to divert us from the goal. We must not run uncertainly (1 Cor. 9:26). Our language must be that of the psalmist who wrote, "Whom have I in heaven but You? And there is none upon earth that I desire besides You" (Ps. 73:25).

Such concentration does not come naturally. It must be developed through rigorous training and ceaseless effort. When we focus our lives in this way, then the routine work of each day, the moments we spend in relaxation, and even the trials and sufferings we experience take on new meaning as they become a part of the things that "work together for good" (Rom. 8:28).

The writer to the Hebrews expressed the same thought when he wrote, "Let us lay aside every weight, and the sin which so easily ensnares us, and let us run with endurance the race that is set before us, looking unto Jesus, the author and finisher of our faith" (12:1–2).

DEVELOP THE DISCIPLINE TO FORGET

Jesus said, "No one, having put his hand to the plow, and looking back, is fit for the kingdom of God" (Luke 9:62). The runner in a race cannot afford to look back. He will lose his speed, lose his direction, and, if he is not careful, lose the race. This is not an easy assignment for any of us. It is the result of a decision we make. We simply decide that we will not be controlled by our past.

Paul was talking about selective forgetfulness. What kind of things need to be forgotten? First of all, we must forget our *failures*. If we look at our past failures as opportunities to learn and grow, then it is all right to remember them. If we allow them to fill us with despair and defeat, we must forget them. In other words, we may allow our failures to teach us but not to terrorize us.

When Sir Winston Churchill visited the United States during World War II, he was heard to say, "If the past quarrels with the past, there can be no future. We must learn to accept the past as unalterable and move on."

Second, we must forget our *successes*. We may remember them if they make us grateful. We must forget them if they make us proud and arrogant. A leader of the persecuted church once said that 95 percent of the believers who face the test of persecution pass it, while 95 percent of the believers who face the test of prosperity fail it. If we keep remembering our successes, we will soon have nothing to remember.

Paul already listed the many things in his past that could have caused him to be proud. He responded to those things in the same way that he responded to his failures. He made a definite decision to forget them. He knew they had no bearing on his standing with Christ!

He was at the zenith of his career, and yet he realized that he had not reached the high-water mark of his calling. He had permeated major cities with the gospel, he had founded churches that continued to flourish, he had written major doctrinal letters that even today astound the scholars, but he was not satisfied with himself. The more he accomplished, the more he saw that needed to be accomplished.

There is a story about a great sculptor who after years of work created a statue so perfectly fashioned that he could discover no line that needed to be retouched, no feature that needed to be remodeled. A friend found the artist in tears. "I shall never do anything better than this," moaned the sculptor. "It is the perfection of my ideal." No one need ever worry of such disappointment in the Christian experience. There is always room to grow in Christ.

DEVELOP THE DISCIPLINE TO FOLLOW

Paul's desire for Christlikeness is presented in Philippians 3:13–14 as a footrace. He used three different athletic expressions that would have been well known to his readers.

The first, "reaching forward," refers to a sporting event. This same apostle, who in verse 9 reminded us that we cannot obtain the righteousness that is from God by our own effort, now tells us that we must make every effort to live the righteous life. In fact, the entire epistle is full of references to the intensity of the Christian life. Paul spoke to the Philippians about "stand[ing] fast" (1:27) and running and laboring (2:16). He held up for admiration the life of Epaphroditus, who for the sake of the gospel was near to death (2:30).

The second word is the verb *apprehend*, which means "to lay hold of" and "to pull down." It is the picture of a football player who runs someone down from behind and tackles him. Paul said he was forging ahead to apprehend Christ, just as Christ had apprehended him on the road to Damascus. He wanted to experience everything that God had for his life, and he was eager to grab hold of all that God put in front of him.

The third expression is Paul's statement that he was "press[ing] toward the goal." The verb *press* denotes an athlete who runs without swerving off course, straining every nerve and muscle as he keeps on running with all his might toward the goal.

For Paul the goal and the prize were one and the same. Though not defined in this passage, this is a clear reference to the many promises that are given to those who are victorious, including the word of commendation from the Lord Jesus Christ (Luke 19:17). It embraces "the crown of righteousness, which the Lord, the righteous Judge, will give ... on that Day" (2 Tim. 4:8). It could refer to what Peter called the "crown of glory that does not fade away" (1 Pet. 5:4). Whatever else, this prize and goal will be more than eye has seen or ear has heard or man has ever contemplated (1 Cor. 2:9).

At the Greek games, the winner of a race was summoned from the stadium floor to the seat of the judge and a wreath of leaves was placed upon his head. In Athens, the winner was also awarded five hundred coins, free meals, and a front-row seat at the theater.

These were coveted goals and prizes, but they were temporary. Our prize is described as "imperishable" (1 Cor. 9:25).

You may feel that the cost is more than you care to pay, the energy more than you desire to put forth. Let me remind you again that the prize of the high calling of God in Christ Jesus is worth more than you could ever give! Once again Vince Lombardi's words about discipline seem appropriate:

> I've never known a man worth his salt who in the long run, deep down in his heart, didn't appreciate the grind, the discipline. There is something in good men that really yearns for discipline. I firmly believe that any man's finest hour—his greatest fulfillment to all he holds dear—is that moment when he has worked his heart out ... and lies exhausted on the field of battle—victorious.[6]

Therefore let us, as many as are mature, have this mind; and if in anything you think otherwise, God will reveal even this to you. Nevertheless, to the degree that we have already attained, let us walk by the same rule, let us be of the same mind.

Brethren, join in following my example, and note those who so walk, as you have us for a pattern. For many walk, of whom I have told you often, and now tell you even weeping, that they are the enemies of the cross of Christ: whose end is destruction, whose god is their belly, and whose glory is in their shame—who set their mind on earthly things. For our citizenship is in heaven, from which we also eagerly wait for the Savior, the Lord Jesus Christ, who will transform our lowly body that it may be conformed to His glorious body, according to the working by which He is able even to subdue all things to Himself.

Philippians 3:15–21

THE JOY OF MATURITY

Philippians 3:15–21

*For our citizenship is in heaven, from which we also
eagerly wait for the Savior, the Lord Jesus Christ.*

In one of the many attempts to scale Mount Everest before the
successful climb in 1953, a team of mountain climbers made a
final dash for the summit. Their courageous attempt failed, and
today they lie buried somewhere in the eternal snow. One of the
party, who had stayed below when the final assault was attempted,
returned to London. One day as he was giving a lecture on mountain climbing, he stood before a magnificent picture of Mount
Everest. As he concluded his lecture, he turned around and,
addressing the mountain, said, "We have tried to conquer you and
failed; we tried again and you beat us; but we shall beat you, for
you cannot grow bigger, but we can."

Just as a true mountain climber can never give up as long as there is still an unconquered peak, so Paul could not let the Philippian believers give up until they had reached maturity. His challenge to them was to keep on walking, keep on growing, keep on climbing until they reached their potential in Christ. He focused his attention on four things that are necessary if believers are to keep moving upward in their Christian experience.

GREAT ENCOURAGEMENT WITHIN US

One of Paul's special gifts was his ability to encourage those around him. He held the standards high and constantly found ways to inspire his followers to continue striving toward their goals.

> Whether or not it was because of his earlier associations with Barnabas (meaning "Son of Encouragement," so named by his colleagues), Paul himself specialized in this ministry. Encouragement is a constantly recurring note in his letters to churches, especially those churches who were passing through fiery trials.[1]

At first, Paul's words seem to be a contradiction. Back in verse 12, Paul had written that he had not attained perfection, and now here in verse 15 (KJV), he exhorted his readers to strive for perfection. How could he expect from them what he had never been able to achieve after a lifetime of climbing?

The answer lies in the word Paul used for "perfection." A form of the Greek word *teleios* is found in verse 12 and also here. It is translated "mature" in verse 15 and has a different sense from that of verse 12, where Paul used the verb form in the perfect tense ("am perfected") to denote absolute spiritual maturity, or sinless perfection. Here the word speaks of relative spiritual maturity. This maturity is not a state of sinless perfection but of completeness, like the maturity of an adult compared with that of an infant. Guy King used this analogy to explain:

> Down on the track, final perfection of the sprint is one hundred yards in ten seconds. You stand with stopwatch in hand, and you gauge him at ten yards in one second—perfect. Not final perfect, but stage perfect. So he goes on perfect at each ten yards, until at the end of the hundred yards, he has reached final perfection in ten seconds. So it is in the New Testament. It is relative. When Our Lord says, "Be ye perfect as I am perfect" (Matt. 5:48), He does not mean that we are expected to achieve divine perfection; but that we are to be perfect in our sphere, and stage, as God is in His.[2]

There are two anticipated responses to Paul's challenge. Those two responses are wrapped up in the phrases "this mind" and "think otherwise."

The people of "this mind" are those who have decided that growth and maturity are important goals for the believer. They acknowledge with Paul that they need to keep pressing toward the mark of spiritual maturity. They have left behind the idea of becoming mature through obeying the law, and they are going on to seek perfection in Christ.

Those who "think otherwise" probably assume they have already arrived at perfection. Perhaps they wanted to grow but would not pay the price of pressing toward that goal. Whatever their philosophy, Paul was not worried, for God would clear it up in His own time. He would reveal to them that Paul was telling the truth. It reminds me of Jesus's promise to the Jews: "If anyone wills to do His will, he shall know concerning the doctrine, whether it is from God or whether I speak on My own authority" (John 7:17).

Paul acknowledged that spiritual progress up to this point had come from following the standards set down in God's Word. He encouraged the Philippians to continue to follow that same rule and that same attitude.

Occasionally during basketball or football playoffs, you will hear a sports announcer talking about a star player who is having a bad day. As the sportscaster explains why this athlete has been allowed to continue, even though he is playing very badly, he might say something like this: "The coach has decided to stay with the man who brought him here." In other words, since this athlete was very responsible for his team's qualifying for the playoffs, it does not make sense to remove him from the game now, even though he is not performing well.

This was Paul's message. What these believers had attained spiritually had come through certain principles and procedures.

They were not to let the legalists change the way they approached the Christian life. Paul's words to the churches in Galatia carried a similar challenge: "Are you so foolish? Having begun in the Spirit, are you now being made perfect by the flesh?" (3:3)

Paul's encouragement was straightforward. The Philippians were to keep on walking the same walk and thinking the same thoughts. The language here is military. They were to stay in line behind the principles of the word of God. They were to walk toward perfection. While we are not held responsible for sinless perfection, Jesus does have that as His goal for us. Listen to C. S. Lewis:

> That is why He warned people to "count the cost" before becoming Christians. "Make no mistake," He says, "If you let Me, I will make you perfect. The moment you put yourself in My hands, that is what you are in for. Nothing less, or other, than that. You have free will, and if you choose, you can push Me away. But if you do not push Me away, understand that I am going to see this job through. Whatever suffering it may cost you in your earthly life … whatever it costs Me, I will never rest, nor let you rest, until you are literally perfect—until My Father can say without reservation that He is well pleased with you, as He said He was well pleased with Me. This I can do and will do. But I will not do anything less."[3]

GODLY EXAMPLES AROUND US

Paul invited the Philippians to "join in following [his] example." Actually the phrase could be translated "become fellow imitators of me." The Greek word is related to our English word *mimics*. Just as Paul mimicked Christ, so they should mimic or imitate him.

The last phrase of Philippians 3:17 speaks of Paul and his friends being examples. The word is the Greek *tupos*, which is best translated by our word *pattern*. It actually means "to strike an exact image upon a blank piece of metal" and was used in Paul's day to speak of making coins. As Paul followed Christ closely, he was making a pattern for others to follow. In his first letter to Timothy, Paul used a form of this same word to describe the role he was to play with those who would come after him: "However, for this reason I obtained mercy, that in me first Jesus Christ might show all longsuffering, as a pattern to those who are going to believe on Him for everlasting life" (1:16).

When Paul said, "You have us for a pattern," he widened the scope of model Christians beyond himself to people like Timothy, Epaphroditus, Silas, and others in Philippi. It is impossible to assess the power of a godly example.

Many years ago someone gave me a column from the *Alliance Witness*. The article, "Secret Weapon in the Classroom," was to encourage Christian teachers to live godly lives. The words made a profound impression on my life.

> In no other profession, save possibly the ministry (which is a form of teaching), does the total character of the individual count for so much.

An immoral person can assemble a good Chevrolet. A salesman can play the horses in off-hours without jeopardizing his client relationships. But a teacher is teaching twenty-four hours a day. His out-of-class contacts with students may, in fact, be the more important. His standing as a teacher depends on a wide variety of assessments.

The teacher is more influential than the subject matter he teaches. The attitude of his students toward the subject matter and the benefit they derive from it will be conditioned largely by their assessment of him as a person.

If those assertions seem too strong, think back to your own formal education…. Apart from the basics of reading, writing and arithmetic, just how much hard knowledge can you recall from the years you spent in the classroom?

Yet you can look back and … recall teachers who … made a lasting mark.[4]

GODLESS ENEMIES AWAY FROM US

The enemies of a mountain climber are usually the elements, such as avalanches, unexpected blizzards, high winds, and uncertain footing. The enemies for a spiritual mountain climber are usually people. Earlier Paul had written of such enemies as "dogs" and "evil workers" (Phil. 3:2). They are the wolves in sheep's clothing that our Lord talked about. These are the ones who "pervert the gospel of Christ" (Gal. 1:7). They pose as friends and practice as foes. Paul wept as he described them in the following terms.

THEIR GOAL—"WHOSE END IS DESTRUCTION"

The word for destruction is *perdition*. Judas was called the "son of perdition" (John 17:12). The true child of God glories in the cross (Gal. 6:14). These are *enemies* of the cross who have the same destiny as the beast of Revelation. They are headed for the lake of fire, the second death. Paul's destination was the prize of the upward calling of God in Christ Jesus. Their end was perdition! Phillips said, "These men are heading for utter destruction."

THEIR GOD—"WHOSE GOD IS THEIR BELLY"

Their appetite is their god. They are not in control of their appetites; rather, their appetites are in control of them. They pander to themselves. Paul had no confidence in the flesh, did not believe he had already arrived, and considered himself far from perfect. But these enemies of the cross took as their god whatever felt good. "For those who are such do not serve our Lord Jesus Christ, but their own belly, and by smooth words and flattering speech deceive the hearts of the simple" (Rom. 16:18).

THEIR GLORY—"WHOSE GLORY IS IN THEIR SHAME"

First they give themselves to indulgence and then they begin to justify their behavior and proclaim that what they do is right and lawful. They are like those the prophet Isaiah described: "Woe to those who call evil good, and good evil; who put darkness for light, and light for darkness; who put bitter for sweet, and sweet for bitter!" (Isa. 5:20).

Their bad conduct is supported by a code that endorses what they are doing. Their sense of values is perverted so that they glory in the things they should be ashamed of. Paul gloried in Christ (Phil. 3:3, 7–12); they glory in their shame. Like professional basketball players who brag about their sexual conquests and like the talk-show host who wrote a book about all the different women he had been with, these enemies brag about things they should be ashamed of.

Please note that these enemies were not distant. They were teachers who were visible to the church of Philippi. Paul said in verse 17 that the Christians were to mark those who lived in such a way. In other words, these examples were close enough to be seen! Most scholars believe they were a part of the church at Philippi. When President Bush appointed Magic Johnson to the commission on AIDS, he remarked that he would be a good member because he was such a great role model for our kids. Unfortunately we have far too many role models like that. Those of us who are parents need to talk to our children about the people they admire!

THEIR GRID—"WHO SET THEIR MIND ON EARTHLY THINGS"

Everyone has a grid or a mind-set through which he or she makes major decisions. That grid determines his or her life. Paul's grid was heaven; theirs was the earth. At the center of their existence was the world (Rom. 12:2). Their minds had not been renewed, and they could not think the things they ought to think. Their view was all soil and no sky.

God leaves us no middle ground here. There is no halfway zone where we may be partial in our commitments. "Friendship with the world is enmity with God" (James 4:4). We are to set our minds "on things above, not on things on the earth" (Col. 3:2). One writer observed, "It is because we are dropping the truths of eternity and immortality and Heaven out of our thinking that we are fast becoming a generation of earthbound pagans."[5]

GRAND EXPECTATION BEFORE US

Malcolm Muggeridge wrote something amazing in *A Twentieth Century Testimony*:

> When I look back on my life nowadays, which I sometimes do, what strikes me most forcibly about it is that what seemed at the time most significant and seductive, seems now most futile and absurd. For instance, success in all of its various guises, being known and being praised; ostensible pleasures, like acquiring money or seducing women, or traveling, going to and fro in the world and up and down in it like Satan, explaining and experiencing whatever *Vanity Fair* has to offer. In retrospect, all these exercises in

self-gratification seem pure fantasy, what Pascal called "licking the earth."[6]

As we have already discovered, Paul set his past behind him and determined to forget it. But he had a clear picture of the future and kept it constantly before him. In his bestseller, *The Seven Habits of Highly Effective People*, Stephen Covey reported that all highly effective people have developed the discipline "to begin with the end in mind."[7] He explained that seeing the goal clearly before one sets out to reach it is the difference between those who achieve their objectives and those who do not.

There was nothing more central to Paul's thinking than the coming of his Savior, and he eagerly awaited that day. He was "looking for the blessed hope and glorious appearing of our great God and Savior Jesus Christ" (Titus 2:13).

The return of Jesus Christ is mentioned in every one of the New Testament books except Galatians, 2 and 3 John, and Philemon. When Paul said we are looking for that blessed hope, he used a Greek word that conveys the idea of eagerness and persistence of expectation. It also suggests total concentration! We are looking away from everything else and to Him. Ralph Herring helps us understand the context in which Paul's words concerning the coming of the Savior would be received:

> The greatest event in any colony of Rome was a visit from the emperor. History records the most elaborate honors for such an occasion. Coins

were struck, new highways were built, magnificent public buildings were erected, and imperial
favors were bestowed by way of celebration.
Looking forward to such an event, the Christian
colony has something infinitely glorious in pros-
pect in the coming of the Lord Jesus Christ.[8]

When Paul called this a *hope*, he was not communicating
uncertainty. The New Testament concept of hope for the believer
is "a sure thing that will happen at an unspecified time." It is
this hope that makes the difference for Christians. After Francis
Schaeffer died, his wife wrote these words that explain the nature
of that hope for all who believe:

It was 4:00 a.m. precisely that a soft last breath
was taken ... and he was absent. That absence
was so sharp and precise! Absent. As for his
presence with the Lord ... I had to turn to my
Bible to know that. I only know that a person
is present with the Lord because the Bible tells
us so. The inerrant Bible became more important
to me than ever before. My husband fought for
truth and fought for the truth of the inspiration
of the Bible—the inerrancy of the Bible—all the
days that I knew him ... through my fifty-two
years of knowing him. But—never have I been
more impressed with the wonder of having a

trustworthy message from God, an unshakable word from God—than right then! I feel very sorry for the people who have to be "hoping without any assurance" … because they don't know what portion of the Bible is myth and what portion might possibly be trusted.[9]

The apostle was excited not only about the *return of Christ* but also about the *redemption of the body*. He reminded the Philippians that when Christ returns, He will "transform our lowly body." The Greeks had a view of the human body that made Paul's promise to the believers even more special:

> By many Greek pagans, the body was viewed as a prison from which at death the soul will be delivered. The body was "intrinsically vile." To Paul, however, the body was a temple, even the sanctuary of the Holy Spirit (1 Cor. 6:19). To be sure, right now, as the result of the entrance of sin, it is the body of humiliation…. As such it is exposed to sin's curse in the form of weakness, suffering, sickness, ugliness, futility, death, but at His coming the Savior—who is a complete Savior—will refashion it in such a manner that this new outward fashion or appearance will truly reflect the new and lasting inner form, for it will have a form like the glorious body of the ascended Lord.[10]

So when Paul used the word *lowly*, he was not depreciating the body. All he was saying is that our earthly bodies are limited. When people ask us how we are doing as we grow older, we answer, "Fine," but it is a relative answer:

> There's nothing whatever the matter with me.
> I'm just as healthy as I can be.
>
> I have arthritis in both my knees,
> And when I talk, I talk with a wheeze.
> My pulse is weak and my blood is thin,
> But I'm awfully well for the shape I'm in.
>
> Arch supports I have for my feet,
> Or I wouldn't be able to be on the street.
>
> And every morning I'm a sight.
> Sleep is denied me, night after night.
>
> My memory is failing, my heart's in a spin,
> I'm practically living on aspirin.
> But I'm awfully well for the shape I'm in.
>
> The moral is, as this tale I unfold,
> That for you and for me, who are growing old,
> It's better to say, I'm fine, with a grin,
> Than to let them know the shape we're in![11]

While we don't know exactly how our bodies are going to be changed in that glorious day, we do know the limitations and pain and suffering and death will be forever gone! To the Corinthians Paul said that our bodies will be buried in decay and raised without decay; they will be sown in humiliation and raised in splendor; they will be sown in weakness and raised in strength; they will be sown a physical body and raised a spiritual body (1 Cor. 15:42–44).

Our new bodies will be like the glorious body of our Lord Jesus Christ. Apart from the resurrection of Jesus Himself, there are only three resurrections recorded in the Gospels: the son of the widow of Nain, the daughter of Jairus, and Lazarus. All these situations began in mourning until Jesus came; then that sorrow was turned into joy and gladness. Jesus said of Himself, "I am the resurrection and the life" (John 11:25). Whenever the life of Jesus meets death, death is always defeated. When He comes again, death will be dealt its final blow. As Paul said to the Corinthians, "Death is swallowed up in victory" (1 Cor. 15:54).

How did Paul know these things were going to happen? How can we be sure? The guarantee is given here as "the working by which He is able even to subdue all things to Himself" (Phil. 3:21). Paul described the power of the Lord in three ways in this closing verse of chapter 3. The word *able* is the translation of the Greek word *dunamai*. The Lord does have the power to accomplish what He has promised. He is able! The word *working* reminds us that His power is on target. He possesses the power, but He also possesses the wisdom to see that His power is utilized in accomplishing His plan. Finally, His power is such as to remove all doubt from our minds. It is this very power that will ultimately subdue all things unto Himself. Alec Motyer described it like this:

> The forces of nature, the ordered universe, the unbelieving hearts of men, spiritual wickedness in heavenly places, the prince of the power of the air: mention any opponent of the return of Christ and Scripture will nullify its opposition by the power that subdues all things.... It is this power which underwrites the promise of His coming again.[12]

As we look back over this section of Paul's letter, we see an obvious contrast between the enemies of the cross and the champions of the cross. Putting these contrasting statements side by side can be very encouraging to those of us who are following the Lord:

> The enemies of the cross are heading for destruction. (v. 19)

> The champions of the cross are waiting for a Savior from heaven. (v. 20)

> The enemies of the cross worship their earthly bodies and its appetites. (v. 19)

The champions of the cross look for the transformation of their earthly body (body of humiliation) into a glorious body. (v. 21)

The enemies of the cross have perverted values and glory in their shame. (v. 19)

The champions of the cross have true values and look forward to the glory of the future. (v. 21)

The enemies of the cross are earthbound. (v. 19)

The champions of the cross are heavenbound. (v. 20)

Whenever we compare the belief systems of the two groups, it is important to look to the very end. As Stephen Covey reminded us, we must "begin with the end in mind." James Montgomery Boice told the story of two men who powerfully illustrate this principle:

In the year 1899, two famous men died in America. One was an unbeliever who had made a career of debunking the Bible and arguing against the Christian doctrines. The other was a Christian. Colonel Ingersoll, after whom the famous Ingersoll lectures on immortality at Harvard University are named, was the unbeliever. His death was sudden and came as an unmitigated shock to his family. His body was kept in the home for several days because Ingersoll's wife could not bear to part with it; and it was finally removed only because the corpse was decaying and the health of the family required it. At length the remains were cremated, and the display at the crematorium was so dismal that some of the scene was even picked up by the newspapers and communicated to the nation at large. Ingersoll had used his great intellect to deny the resurrection. When death came there was no hope, and the departure was received by his friends and family as an uncompensated tragedy.

In the same year the evangelist Dwight L. Moody died, and his death was triumphant for himself and his family. Moody had been declining for some time, and his family had taken turns being with him. On the morning of his death his son, who was standing by the bedside, heard him exclaim, "Earth is receding; heaven is opening; God is calling." "You are dreaming, Father," his son said. Moody answered, "No, Will, this is no dream. I have been within the gates. I have seen the children's faces." For a while it seemed as if Moody was reviving, but he began to slip away again. He said, "Is this death? This is not bad; there is no valley. This is bliss. This is glorious." By this time his daughter was present, and she began to pray for his recovery. He said, "No, no, Emma, don't pray for that. God is calling. This is my coronation day. I have been looking forward to it." Shortly after that Moody was received into heaven. At the funeral his family and friends joined in a joyful service. They spoke and sang hymns. They heard the words proclaimed, "Where, O death, is your victory? Where, O death, is your sting? The sting of death is sin; and the power of sin is the law. But thanks be to God! He gives us the victory through our Lord Jesus Christ" (1 Cor. 15:55–57). Moody's death was a part of that victory.[13]

Therefore, my beloved and longed-
for brethren, my joy and crown, so
stand fast in the Lord, beloved.

I implore Euodia and I implore Syntyche
to be of the same mind in the Lord. And I
urge you also, true companion, help these
women who labored with me in the gospel,
with Clement also, and the rest of my fellow
workers, whose names are in the Book of Life.

Rejoice in the Lord always.
Again I will say, rejoice!

Let your gentleness be known to all
men. The Lord is at hand.

Philippians 4:1–5

THE JOY OF HARMONY

Philippians 4:1–5

Rejoice in the Lord always. Again I will say, rejoice!

Recently I came across a prescription for unhappiness that I believe has been the philosophy of several people I know. If you are looking for a new way to be unhappy, perhaps one or two of these ideas will motivate you to greater depths of despair:

1. Make little things bother you; don't just let them, *make* them.
2. Lose your perspective of things, and keep it lost. Don't put first things first.
3. Get yourself a good worry—one about which you cannot do anything but worry.
4. Be a perfectionist: Condemn yourself and others for not achieving perfection.

5. Be right, always right, perfectly right all the time. Be the only one who is right and be rigid about your rightness.

6. Don't trust or believe people, or accept them at anything but their worst and weakest. Be suspicious. Impute ulterior motives to them.

7. Always compare yourself unfavorably to others, which is the guarantee of instant misery.

8. Take personally, with a chip on your shoulder, everything that happens to you that you don't like.

9. Don't give yourself wholeheartedly or enthusiastically to anyone or to anything.

10. Make unhappiness the aim of your life, instead of bracing for life's barbs through a "bitter with the sweet" philosophy.[1]

Follow this prescription faithfully for two weeks and I guarantee you unhappiness. Of course, most normal people do not start out with a goal of unhappiness! But many, including some Christians, seem to arrive at that station anyway. If you happen to be one who struggles with a general feeling of unhappiness, Paul's words in these five verses are directed to you in a very personal way. He offers no new ideas about happiness, but what he does offer is a philosophy of life that promises to bring you lasting joy.

Paul's "therefore" in verse 1 connects us again to the great hope that awaits us in the coming again of our Lord Jesus Christ. "Therefore," said the apostle, "since you have such a great hope, don't let anything destroy the firm foundation upon which that hope is resting."

In this last chapter of Philippians, Paul moves away from his explanation of the great purposes of God in Christ and begins to exhort the believers to live in a way that is in keeping with the great truths they have been taught. In the early church there were men who had the title of "exhorter." These men were gifted pastor-teachers, and they used their gift of exhortation to encourage and motivate their listeners toward holiness in their walk with the Lord. The church today has developed skill in analyzing and criticizing but could learn much from the early exhorters. According to the writer of Hebrews, we ought to be getting better at exhortation as the time of our Lord's return draws nigh: "Not forsaking the assembling of ourselves together, as is the manner of some, but *exhorting one another*, and so much the more as you see the Day approaching" (10:25). Here are Paul's four exhortations.

DON'T BE DEFEATED

Paul said five things about these Philippian believers as he prepared to challenge them. They were first of all "brethren." These people were family to the apostle, and he considered them his spiritual brothers and sisters. Second, twice in the same verse, he called them "beloved." Third, he described them as "longed-for." More than anything else, he valued the people themselves. Fourth, he described them as his "joy." This is just what he called the Thessalonian believers: "For what is our hope, or joy, or crown of rejoicing? Is it not even you in the presence of our Lord Jesus Christ at His coming?" (1 Thess. 2:19). Finally, he referred to them as his "crown." Paul looked ahead to the judgment seat of Christ and knew his faithfulness toward these Philippian believers would be rewarded by the Lord Jesus Christ. Earlier in his letter he had exhorted them to hold "fast the word of life, so that I may rejoice in the day of Christ that I have not run in vain or labored in vain" (2:16).

Paul's words of endearment are reminiscent of his opening remarks in 1:1–11. He really cared about these Philippians and did not want them to lose heart and give in to the pressure of their enemies. He urged them to "stand fast in the Lord" (4:1). The expression "in the Lord" is found eight times in this epistle (1:14; 2:19, 24, 29; 3:1; 4:1–2, 4).

At first it may seem as if Paul has contradicted himself. In chapter 3 he told the Philippians to run; now he is telling them to stand. There is no contradiction! In the matters of growth and service, they must be always running and pressing toward the mark. But in matters of faith and loyalty to Jesus Christ, they must be ready to stand.

It is intriguing that the believers were not told to march forward into battle. They were told to stand. In every one of the Pauline letters, believers were not instructed in offensive warfare. Even in Ephesians 6 the instruction was to take the whole armor of God so that they might stand. The fact is, there is no more ground to take. Jesus Christ already won the battle decisively when He died on the cross and was resurrected from the dead. His command to us is to hold the ground that He has already won. We are to stand fast "in the Lord." Watchman Nee, the Chinese evangelist, gives some helpful words on this:

The difference between defensive and offensive warfare is this, that in the former I have got the ground and only seek to keep it, whereas in the latter, I have not got the ground and am fighting in order to get it. And that is precisely the difference between the warfare waged by the Lord Jesus and the warfare waged by us. His was offensive; ours is, in essence, defensive. He warred against Satan in order to gain the victory. Through the cross he carried that warfare to the very threshold of Hell itself, to lead forth his captivity captive. Today we war against Satan only to maintain and consolidate the victory which he has already gained. By the resurrection God proclaimed his Son victor over the whole realm of darkness and the ground Christ won he has given to us. We do not need to fight to obtain it. We only need to hold it against all challengers.[2]

DON'T BE DIVISIVE

There is little hope for the church to *stand* if it is divided with disharmony and friction. When Paul came to Philippi to start the work there, he met first on a Sunday with a group of women who had gathered at the river to pray. Lydia, the seller of purple, quietly accepted the Lord and began to live for Him (Acts 16:14, 40). Paul owed a debt to the many women who had enough faith to pray and enough courage to stay by the work in its early days. As we examine the history of Christendom, it is hard to imagine where the church of Jesus Christ might be today were it not for the powerful influence that has been wielded by women:

> … the sons they have trained … the services they
> have rendered … the songs they have written …
> the supplications they have offered—from Eunice's
> training of Timothy (2 Tim. 1:5; 3:15); from Mary's
> song of Magnificat (Luke 1:46); from the women
> joining in the Upper Room prayer meeting (Acts
> 1:14) … from these onward, the Church has owed
> a debt she can never adequately repay for all her
> women's sacrifices, service, and sympathy.[3]

However, the Philippian church, which had been started by women, was now being torn apart because of two women. Euodia and Syntyche must have been prominent women in the fellowship. Paul referred to them as "women who labored with me in the gospel." Their effect on the congregation could not be explained apart from some influential standing in the congregation, but they obviously were not living up to their names. Euodia means "sweet fragrance," and Syntyche means "affable." So disruptive was the controversy between these two that someone has suggested that if the Philippians were Paul's crown, Euodia and Syntyche had become two thorns in that crown!

The apostle had been reminding the Philippians throughout this letter that they should be unified. He prayed for them in chapter 1 that their love for one another "may abound still more and more"

(v. 9). In that same chapter he exhorted them to "stand fast in one spirit, with one mind" (v. 27). Then in chapter 2, he told them to be "of one accord, of one mind" (v. 2). In chapter 3 he said, "Let us walk by the same rule, let us be of the same mind" (v. 16). Now, in chapter 4, we find out why he kept repeating the message of unity. Paul knew, as we must, that even the smallest irritations in a church body can grow to major disunity.

In *The Great Divorce*, C. S. Lewis paints a picture of a fictional hell where the major pain is related to fragmented relationships. He has one of the residents of hell say this:

> The trouble is that they're so quarrelsome. As soon as anyone arrives, he settles in some street. Before he's been there twenty-four hours, he quarrels with his neighbour. Before the week is over, he's quarreled so badly that he decides to move. Very likely he finds the next street empty because all the people there have quarreled with their neighbours—and moved.[4]

Anyone who has felt the pain of violent church arguments knows that Lewis is not exaggerating when he identifies the whole process with hell.

As he attempted to deal with the division, Paul called upon his friends in the church to "help these women." He wanted the problem resolved! His appeal was strong and his reasoning was clear. These were members of the body of Christ, and they should not be divided!

When Paul appealed to his "true companion" to step in and try to resolve the problem, he may have been referring to a specific member of the church. "Companion" is the translation of the Greek word *syzygus*. William Hendriksen thinks Paul was using a play on words:

> In all probability … the apostle is making use of a play on a name, for Syzygus means Yokefellow, a person who pulls well in a harness for two, and Paul is saying that Syzygus was true to his name…. It is safe to infer that Syzygus, about whom we have no further information, was one of Paul's comrades or associates in the work of the gospel. When this letter was written he was a prominent member of the church at Philippi, a man of influence who was highly esteemed by his people. Like the apostle himself, he must have been a man of extraordinary tact. Otherwise Paul would not have requested him to lend a hand in restoring harmony between the two women.[5]

Paul appealed to a threefold unity to bring these two women back together:

UNITY IN SALVATION

Paul had already called the Philippians his dearly beloved brethren; now he reminded them again that they were citizens of heaven with their names all written down in the Book of Life. When John referred to the Book of Life in Revelation 20, he said, "Anyone not found written in the Book of Life was cast into the lake of fire" (v. 15). While there is some controversy surrounding the interpretation of this verse, many would agree with what I have written about the Book of Life in *Escape the Coming Night*:

> This Book is an amazing record. It will contain the name of every single person born into the world. If, by the time a person dies, he has not received God's provision of sacrifice to remove his sin, his name will be blotted out of the pages.... As each person steps forward, God will open the various books pointing out what was required to have been accepted as a child of God. When He solemnly opens the Book of Life and begins to look down this immense directory for the person's name, His gentle hands will turn the pages, wishing to find the name of the accused.[6]

Paul's assertion that the names Euodia and Syntyche were recorded in the Book of Life was his way of affirming their standing as fellow believers in the body of Christ.

UNITY IN SPIRIT

When Paul exhorted these two women to be of the same mind, he was referring to the spirit of servanthood and humility that he championed so often throughout this book. If we have that spirit within us, there can never be disunity.

UNITY IN SERVICE

Euodia and Syntyche are wonderfully described here as "these women who labored with me in the gospel, with Clement also, and the rest of my fellow workers." They were not just women who *knew* the Lord; they were women who *served* the Lord. Alec Motyer wrote vividly about this special unity:

> Where there is agreement as to what the Gospel is
> and what ought to be done with it, there is no room
> for personal disagreement. The one ought to exclude
> the other…. To agree on what the Gospel demands
> in its proclamation to the world is to cement unity
> by common action. The singleness of the task ought
> to be reflected in the singleness of the workers.[7]

DON'T BE DISCOURAGED

Perhaps the spirits of the Philippian believers were down. Outside pressure from the enemies of the cross and now division on the inside had them discouraged. So Paul told them, "Rejoice." In this letter the word *rejoice* is used nine times, the word *joy* four times, and the phrase "rejoice with" twice. It is the same message Paul gave to the Thessalonians: "Rejoice always" (1 Thess. 5:16).

There is an old Chinese proverb that says, "If you wish to be happy for one hour, get intoxicated. If you wish to be happy for three days, get married. If you wish to be happy for eight days, kill your pig and eat it. If you wish to be happy forever, learn to fish."

A young man went to a renowned doctor in Paris complaining of depression and asked what he could do to get well. The doctor thought of a well-known man named Grimaldi, a leader of café society who cut a wide and lighthearted swath through Paris night life. The doctor told the young man, "Introduce yourself to Grimaldi. Let him show you how to enjoy yourself and you will get well." The downcast young patient looked up with a sad smile and said, "Doctor, I am Grimaldi."

When Paul exhorted the Philippians to rejoice, he was not motivating them to seek happiness. Joy is not happiness! Joy is a relationship. One of the best definitions of joy that I ever read goes like this: "Joy is the flag flown high from the castle of my heart, for the King is in residence there." This concept of joy centered in God finds its roots in the Old Testament:

> But let all those rejoice who put their trust in You;
> let them ever shout for joy, because You defend
> them; let those also who love Your name be joyful
> in You. (Ps. 5:11)

> I will praise You, O Lord, with my whole heart; I
> will tell of all Your marvelous works. I will be glad
> and rejoice in You; I will sing praise to Your name,
> O Most High. (Ps. 9:1–2)

> The joy of the Lord is your strength. (Neh. 8:10)

The atheist Voltaire once said that men are "tormented atoms in a bit of mud, devoured by death, a mockery of fate. This world, this theater of pride and wrong, swarms with sick fools who talk of happiness."[8]

Happiness is the world's cheap imitation of Christian joy. Happiness is dependent on happenings, on hap, which is another word for "luck." Someone who is hapless is luckless.

When we have joy, it can be our constant possession because it does not depend on the circumstances of the day. Paul said, "Rejoice in the Lord." This philosophy made it possible for him to endure all kinds of problems and still move forward in his walk with Christ. When he wrote his second letter to the church at Corinth, he listed just a few of the things he had endured. Now we know how he endured them. He had the strength of genuine joy in his life:

> From the Jews five times I received forty stripes minus one. Three times I was beaten with rods; once I was stoned; three times I was shipwrecked; a night and a day I have been in the deep; in journeys often, in perils of waters, in perils of robbers, in perils of my own countrymen, in perils of the Gentiles, in perils in the city, in perils in the wilderness, in perils in the sea, in perils among false brethren; in weariness and toil, in sleeplessness often, in hunger and thirst, in fastings often, in cold and nakedness—besides the other things, what comes upon me daily: my deep concern for all the churches. (11:24–28)

How could any one man experience all these things and still have the spirit of joy? Paul understood what most modern men do not, that joy and pain are often compatible emotions. One of my favorite authors, Lewis Smedes, explains:

> You and I were created for joy, and if we miss it, we miss the reason for our existence.… If our joy is honest joy, it must somehow be congruous with human tragedy. This is the test of joy's integrity: is it compatible with pain? … Only the heart that hurts has a right to joy.[9]

Another writer adds an even more powerful dimension to this thought:

> One of the most common obstacles to celebrating life fully is our avoidance of pain. We dread pain. We fear pain. We do anything to escape pain. Our culture reinforces our avoidance of pain by assuring us that we can live a painless life.… But to live without pain is to live half-alive … pain and joy run together. When we cut ourselves off from pain, we have unwittingly cut ourselves off from joy as well.[10]

Earlier in this letter, Paul spoke of the things "which happened to me" (1:12). That whole section explains how God used the difficult things that happened in Paul's life! In the midst of that situation, Paul twice acknowledged his joy (1:18). The apostle James also understood the connection between joy and pain. He wrote, "My brethren, count it all joy when you fall into various trials" (1:2).

In one of the most encouraging passages in the Old Testament, the prophet Habakkuk validated this concept of joy:

> Though the fig tree may not blossom, nor fruit be
> on the vines; though the labor of the olive may fail,
> and the fields yield no food; though the flock may
> be cut off from the fold, and there be no herd in the
> stalls—yet I will rejoice in the LORD, I will joy in the
> God of my salvation. (3:17–18)

DON'T BE DEFENSIVE

When the apostle urged the Philippians to let their gentleness be known to all men, he used a word that means "to be reasonable, to not be carried away with an obsession about unimportant matters to the point of fighting over nonessentials." Paul was exhorting his friends to avoid that inflexible attitude that will not bend or yield to another's opinion. He was not saying that doctrinal convictions should be yielded; he was not urging compromise. Paul's exhortation was a very proper ending to this whole discussion. We must cultivate the right spirit toward one another so that even in areas where we may not see eye to eye, we can still love one another and avoid the problems that separated Euodia and Syntyche.

William Hendriksen describes this quality as "big-heartedness." Here is what he means by that term:

The lesson which Paul teaches is that true bless-edness cannot be obtained by the person who rigorously insists on whatever he regards as his just due. The Christian is the man who reasons that it is far better to suffer wrong than to inflict wrong (1 Cor. 6:7). Sweet reasonableness is an essential ingredient of true happiness. Now such big-heart-edness, such forbearance, the patient willingness to yield wherever yielding is possible without violating any real principle, must be shown to all, not only to fellow believers.[11]

The final reminder, "The Lord is at hand," takes us back to the end of chapter 3 where Paul spoke of eagerly waiting for the coming of the Lord. Now he reminds us that the Lord's coming is at hand. I think he is providing us with another good test for the issues that separate us. If the Lord is at hand, what about our petty concerns? As we look back, here are Paul's four principles for continued harmony:

1. Don't be defeated—stand.
2. Don't be divisive—be of the same mind.
3. Don't be discouraged—rejoice in the Lord.
4. Don't be defensive—let your big-heartedness be known to all men.

Since we began this chapter with some cynical principles for leading an unhappy life, I'd like to conclude with something I read in Judson Edwards's book *What They Never Told Us about How to Get Along with Each Other*. Here are six rules that will go a long way toward making our fellowship sweet and our divisions few:

1. Agree More … Argue Less
2. Listen More … Talk Less
3. Produce More … Advertise Less
4. Confess More … Accuse Less
5. Laugh More … Fret Less
6. Give More … Receive Less[12]

These six axioms seem right at home alongside Paul's letter, and I would suggest you keep them around where you can look at them once in a while! For whatever we do to promote harmony among God's children is near to the heart of our Savior, who drew a straight line between our love for one another and joy:

These things I have spoken to you, that My joy may remain in you, and that your joy may be full. This is My commandment, that you love one another as I have loved you. (John 15:11–12)

My friend Tim Hansel tells a story that captures the essence of harmony and teamwork that I have tried to describe in this chapter:

Jimmy Durante, one of the great entertainers of a generation ago … was asked to be a part of a show for World War II veterans. He told them his schedule was very busy and he could afford only a few minutes, but if they wouldn't mind his doing one short monologue and immediately leaving for his next appointment, he would come. Of course the show's director agreed happily.

But when Jimmy got on stage, something interesting happened. He went through the short monologue and then stayed. The applause grew louder and louder and he kept staying. Pretty soon, he had been on thirty minutes. Finally he took a last bow and left the stage. Backstage someone stopped him and said, "I thought you had to go after a few minutes. What happened?"

Jimmy answered, "I did have to go, but I can show you the reason I stayed. You can see for yourself if you'll look down on the front row." In the front row were two men, each of whom had lost an arm in the war. One had lost his right arm and the other had lost his left. Together, they were able to clap, and that's exactly what they were doing, loudly and cheerfully.[13]

Be anxious for nothing, but in everything by prayer
and supplication, with thanksgiving, let your
requests be made known to God; and the peace
of God, which surpasses all understanding, will
guard your hearts and minds through Christ Jesus.

Finally, brethren, whatever things are true,
whatever things are noble, whatever things are
just, whatever things are pure, whatever things are
lovely, whatever things are of good report, if there is
any virtue and if there is anything praiseworthy—
meditate on these things. The things which you
learned and received and heard and saw in me,
these do, and the God of peace will be with you.

Philippians 4:6–9

THE JOY OF SECURITY

Philippians 4:6–9

Be anxious for nothing, but in everything by prayer and supplication, with thanksgiving, let your requests be made known to God.

Tom Landry, the first coach of the Dallas Cowboys football team, is one of my favorite people. When he began to coach the Cowboys, I was just getting started in my seminary program at Dallas Theological Seminary. I attended many of the weekly football luncheons and came to admire Landry as a coach and as a fellow believer in Jesus Christ. One of Coach Landry's great gifts was his ability to keep calm in the midst of battle. The television cameras often showed him standing on the sidelines with his arms folded, seeming very relaxed, while out on the field the game was hanging in the balance. In one of his written testimonies, he revealed the secret of his composure under pressure. He said:

> Most of the athletes who fail to become win-
> ners are those athletes whose fears and anxieties
> prevent them from reaching their potential. I
> overcame my fears and anxieties by a commit-
> ment to something far greater than winning a
> football game—a commitment to Jesus Christ.[1]

Landry is right! The answer to fear and anxiety is a commitment to Jesus Christ. But as we will see in this next section of
Philippians, even Christians can suffer from fear and anxiety.

Because of their status as citizens of a Roman colony, the
Philippian Christians were certainly candidates for anxiety. The
persecution from Nero was beginning to boil and the effects
were starting to be felt all over the Roman domain. These young
Christians knew they would soon be tested for their walk with God.

Even though Paul devoted only four verses to this subject,
he diagnosed the problem, prescribed a cure, recommended a
program, and made a promise to the Philippians. What he said
to them has been a source of great encouragement to all who are
prone to let their fears and anxieties take control of their lives.

THE PROBLEM: WORRY

The New Testament word for *worry* is translated "take thought"
and "be careful" in the King James Version. The word *worry* comes
from the Greek word *merimnao,* which is a combination of two
words: *merizo,* which means "to divide," and *nous,* which means
"mind." So to worry is to have a mind divided between legitimate

thoughts and destructive thoughts. No wonder James said a double-minded man is "unstable in all his ways" (1:8).

The word *anxious* that Paul used is a synonym for our word *worry*. It is the same word Jesus used when He told Martha that she was "worried and troubled about many things" (Luke 10:41). Our Lord also used this word in talking with His disciples when He told them they were to "take no thought" about food, drink, clothing, or shelter (Matt. 6:25 KJV). Obviously He was not suggesting they should never think about such things; rather, He was reminding them that they should not worry about them.

When worry takes over in our lives, it chokes out the word of God (Matt. 13:7, 22). It causes us to abandon our trust in the Lord, who tells us to cast all our cares upon Him (1 Pet. 5:7). I read about a French soldier in World War I who carried into battle a prescription for worry:

> Of two things one is certain. Either you are at the front, or you are behind the lines. If you are at the front, of two things one is certain. Either you are exposed to danger, or you are in a safe place. If you are exposed to danger, of two things one is certain. Either you are wounded, or you are not wounded. If you are wounded, of two things one is certain. Either you recover, or you die. If you recover, there is no need to worry. If you die, you can't worry.[2]

While that seems like a rather fatalistic approach to the problem, it coincides with numerous studies that have been done on the subject. Forty percent of the things people worry about never happen. Thirty percent of the worries are related to past matters that are now beyond the person's control. Twelve percent have to do with anxiety about health, even though there is no illness except in the imagination. Ten percent is worry about friends or neighbors, even though in most cases, there is no reason for the anxiety. Just 8 percent of the worries seem to have some basis in reality. What this means is that most of the things we worry about never happen! The poets who wrote these words were very accurate in their assessments:

> Some of your hurts you have cured,
> And the sharpest you still have survived.
> But what torment of grief you've endured,
> From hurts that have never arrived.

> Most things that make us sigh and fret,
> Are things that haven't happened yet.

Have you heard the story of the nervous clock? Like any good clock, it had been ticking away for years, two ticks per second every day. But one day the clock began to worry about its responsibilities—all those ticks it had to tick. It had to tick 120 ticks a minute, 7,200 ticks an hour, 172,800 ticks per day,

1,209,600 ticks per week! "That's more than 62 million ticks a year!" the clock cried, and it promptly had a nervous breakdown.

The sick clock went to a psychiatrist and explained its troubles. "All those ticks—I don't see how I can stand it!"

The psychiatrist said, "Wait a minute. How many ticks must you tick at a time?"

"Oh, I just tick one tick at a time," the clock replied.

"You go home," the doctor said, "and think about ticking only one tick. And until you have ticked that tick, don't even think about the next tick."

Years ago I clipped this bit of poetry from a magazine, and it has helped me more than once to realize the importance of living one day at a time:

God broke our years into hours and days,
That hour by hour and day by day,
Just going on a little way,
We might be able, all along,
To keep quite strong.

Should all the weight of life be laid
Across our shoulders at just one place,
And the future, rife with woe and struggle,
Meet us face to face,
We could not go;
Our feet would stop, and so
God lays a little on us every day.

> And never, I believe in all life's way,
> Will burdens bear so deep,
> Or pathways lie so steep,
> But we can go, if, by God's power,
> We only bear the burden of the hour.[3]

THE PRESCRIPTION: PRAYER

Here is a marvelous contrast! In nothing be anxious; in everything by prayer, let your requests be made known unto God. Everything is included in prayer that it might be excluded from care. We are not to be careful but prayerful!

A 1992 issue of *Newsweek* gave front-cover prominence to the importance of prayer. The feature article told of a renewed interest in prayer. Citing a recent research project on the subject, the study reported:

> Seventy-eight percent of all Americans pray at least once a week; more than half (57 percent) report praying at least once a day.... Even among the 13 percent of the Americans who claim to be atheists or agnostics, nearly one in five still prays daily.[4]

As to the apparent resurgence of prayer, the following explanation was given:

> In allegedly rootless, materialistic, self-centered America, there is also a hunger for a personal

experience of God that prayer seeks to satisfy.... Serious prayer usually begins after the age of thirty, when the illusion that we are masters of our own fate fades and adults develop a deeper need to call on the Master of the Universe. In an age of relativism, God remains for many the one true absolute. In an era of transience and divorce, God can be the only place left to turn for unconditional love.[5]

It is not new truth to many of us that prayer is a great comfort in uneasy times and a mighty warrior against worry. I am convinced, however, that we are confused about the way prayer actually works for us in such stressful and difficult days. Does Paul's call to prayer mean that when we pray, all the things we worry about will be straightened out for us and that our trouble will be gone? Not necessarily! During World War II, an army chaplain wrote an article on prayer that should abolish any such lingering notion. The article was entitled "Some Pray and Die":

Is there such a thing as getting the "breaks" in prayer? What about the fellows who pray regularly, but get killed regularly? ... I wish people would stop writing about the soldiers who pray and have their prayers answered by *not* getting killed. Why do all the other soldiers seem to get the wrong answer?

What I want to know is this: what sort of an extra special, superpowered prayer is needed to make everything turn out the way you want it? That sounds facetious, almost irreverent, but I'm really serious. I really want to know. I'm an army chaplain, and I could use some special prayers with my men—and heaven knows, we need them badly at times. Because the fact is there are always more men who pray to come back than there are men who get back. Quite a lot more. What is the deciding factor?

The thing for all of us to remember is this: someone else does the answering.... What you have in mind may not be what God has in mind. If you ask Him something, you must be willing to take what He gives.... That is why I am a bit depressed by the writings of those who try to get other people to pray by telling them that you get what you want. People must learn to want what they get.... When I talk to soldiers about prayer, I try to tell them that they must be adults. God expects us to be men. Only children demand a happy ending to every story. How old must we be before we begin to realize that even prayer can't get us everything we want, unless the thing we want is right for us to have?

Who gets the breaks in prayers? Nobody. There is no such thing. We get what God in His infinite love and foreknowledge sees fit to give. That's not always the same as getting what we want. But it ought to be.[6]

If prayer does not always change our situation so that it no longer worries us, then what is the value of praying? Here is the answer! Prayer does not always change the situation and make it better, but prayer always changes us and makes us better.

Prayer, especially prayer accompanied by thanksgiving, is the perfect answer to a heart that is overridden with anxiety:

> In prayer, anxiety is resolved by trust in God. That which causes the anxiety is brought to the One who is totally competent and in whose hands the matter may be left. In thanksgiving, anxiety is resolved by the deliberate acceptance of the worrying circumstance as something which an all-wise, all-loving and all-sovereign God has appointed. Prayer takes up the anxiety-provoking question "How?"—How shall I cope?—and answers by pointing away to Him, to His resources and promises. Thanksgiving addresses itself to the worrying question "Why?"— Why has this happened to me?—and answers by pointing to the great Doer of all who never acts purposelessly and whose purposes never fail.[7]

Norman B. Harrison adds this:

> The world worries, and has ample reason for doing so. It faces tremendous problems, with no real solution for them. But the Christian is

very differently situated. He is "not of the world."
Prayer maintains an other-worldly viewpoint,
and he is spared the mental contagion.[8]

Please note that Paul used four different words for prayer in
verse 6.

- *Prayer* is a general word for offering up our
  desires to God. It describes any form of rever-
  ent address directed to the Father, and it points
  to the frame of mind required in the petitioner.
- *Supplication* comes from a Greek word meaning "entreaty" and pictures the petitioner as a
  subject who comes humbly to his Master with
  a need that must be met. The verb form of this
  word in the original means "to want."
- *Requests* stands for particular items on our
  prayer agenda.
- *Thanksgiving* is the fourth word. Observe the
  change in the connectives that join the words
  together. Between the words *prayer* and *supplication* is the connective *and*. Between the words
  supplication and *thanksgiving* you will find the
  word *with*. This is a subtle reminder that all
  prayer is to be accompanied by the spirit of
  gratitude. Thanksgiving reflects the humble
  attitude of the petitioner. It demonstrates that

the prayer is being offered from a submissive heart. In all prayer, we are to be thankful.

Certainly Paul set the example here. His heart was forever bursting forth in anthems of thankful praise. He taught the Ephesian church that thanksgiving is the product of a Spirit-filled life: "Be filled with the Spirit ... giving thanks always for all things to God the Father in the name of our Lord Jesus Christ" (5:18, 20).

The Christian life is composed of three circles. You can draw them in your imagination. First, the *Worry Circle* in which is "nothing." Second, the *Prayer Circle* into which must be brought "everything." Third, the *Thanksgiving Circle* that must be filled with "anything" that gratitude calls to mind.

In other words, we must be careful for nothing, prayerful for everything, and thankful for anything. Worry is unproductive, and prayer never fails to produce!

Worry? Why worry? What can worry do?
It never keeps a trouble from overtaking you.
It gives you indigestion, and
wakeful hours at night,
And fills with gloom the days,
however fair and bright.
It puts a frown upon the face,
and sharpness in the tone.
We're unfit to live with others,
and unfit to live alone.

Worry? Why worry? What can worry do?
It never keeps a trouble from overtaking you.
Pray? Why pray? What can praying do?
Praying really changes things, arranges life anew.
It's good for your digestion, gives
peaceful sleep at night,
And fills the grayest, gloomiest day with
rays of glowing light.
It puts a smile upon your face, and a
love note in your tone,
Makes you fit to live with others,
and fit to live alone.
Pray? Why Pray? What can praying do?
It brings God down from heaven,
to live and work *with* you.

THE PROGRAM: RIGHT THINKING AND RIGHT ACTION

When anxious thoughts are removed by prayer and thanksgiving, they must surely be replaced with something. Here is Paul's program for continued carefree living.

TO AVOID ANXIETY WE MUST THINK PROPER THOUGHTS

Years ago, plastic surgeon Maxwell Maltz wrote a now-famous book titled *Psycho-Cybernetics*. In the book he tells the story of his own experience with plastic-surgery patients who underwent facial transformations. What surprised Maltz most was the difficulty with which his patients changed their image of themselves after the operation. Even after a disfigured, ugly creature was made over into a beautiful specimen of human flesh, Maltz noticed that the patient's inward picture of himself did not change right away.

In his attempt to explain this phenomenon, Maltz did the research that resulted in the publication of his book. He discovered that the mind has tremendous power to control behavior. He learned that changing the face was not enough. If the mental picture that a person had of himself did not change in correspondence with the surgery, the patient would be left in misery, even though he had spent thousands of dollars to be altered outwardly.[9]

Whether he knew it or not, Maltz was echoing the words of the writer of Proverbs, who said, "As he thinks in his heart, so is he" (23:7). I remember reading a poster that said it this way: "You are not what you think you are; but what you think—you are."

The word Paul used for "thinking" is the Greek word *logizomai*, which means "to ponder, to consider, to give proper weight and value to, to meditate upon."

The apostle gave the Philippians six guidelines for proper meditation and thought. If they would think on these things, they would win over worry!

Guideline one: whatever things are true. The inability to cope with truth is a form of mental illness. Paul urged the Philippians to think thoughts that are true, genuine, and sincere. These reflections must be true to God, true to others, and true to oneself. John Henry Jowett pointed out the nature of this truth when he wrote,

"Truth in a police court is correspondence with fact. Truth in the New Testament is correspondence with God."[10]

When one thinks on things that are not true, it is not long before his life reflects the falsehood he has embraced with his mind.

Guideline two: whatever things are noble. We are to think on things that are honorable, things that claim respect. If it is true that we externalize our thoughts, then honorable people are the result of honorable thoughts! Our thoughts should include only that which is worthy of God. When Paul wrote to Timothy that believers were to lead quiet and peaceable lives in all godliness and honesty (1 Tim. 2:2), he used the same word.

Guideline three: whatever things are just. Things that are just are righteous by both divine and human standards.

Guideline four: whatever things are pure. Living in the impure environment of Philippi, the Philippians would have to fill their minds with pure thoughts in order to combat the unclean influences in their culture. Peter told his readers, "Gird up the loins of your mind" (1 Pet. 1:13).

Purity is one of the consistent themes of the New Testament. Paul wrote, "Do not lay hands on anyone hastily, nor share in other people's sins; keep yourself pure" (1 Tim. 5:22). John wrote, "And everyone who has this hope in Him purifies himself, just as He is pure" (1 John 3:3).

Guideline five: whatever things are lovely. This is the only place where this word *lovely* appears in the New Testament. It was often found in the epitaphs of Paul's day, and it spoke of being pleasing and orderly. It was a term that could be used to describe fine art or music. A thorough reading of 1 Corinthians 13 would give great insight into the meaning of this term. It is the opposite of the confusion and disorder that so often rule in our day.

Guideline six: whatever things are of good report. The words *good report* come from two words meaning "fair speaking." This describes that which is appealing. Listening to such reports builds one up spiritually. Such thoughts are the opposite of filthiness, foolish talking, and coarse jesting (Eph. 5:4).

Each of these six thoughts is characterized by virtue and praise. Warren Wiersbe said, "If it has virtue, it will motivate us to do better; and if it has praise, it is worth commending to others."[11]

R. Kent Hughes, in his book *Disciplines of a Godly Man*, reminds us that this kind of thinking is a matter of choice for each of us:

> Each of Paul's ingredients is explicitly positive. The true, the noble, the right, the pure, the lovely, the admirable all defy negative exposition. Each ingredient was, and is, a matter of personal choice—and our choices make all the difference in the world. We all can choose a thought program which will produce a Christian mind. I have great sympathy for those whose past has been a series of bad choices. I understand that if over the years one has chosen the impure and the illusory and the negative, it is very difficult to change. But as a biblical thinker, I give no quarter to myself or anyone else who rationalizes his present choices by

the past. Brothers, we are free to have a Christian mind. It is within our reach, and it is our duty.

As we consider how Paul's program should affect our minds, the sheer weight of its positives demands a determined rejection of negative input: "Finally, brothers, whatever is untrue, whatever is ignoble, whatever is wrong, whatever is impure, whatever is unlovely, whatever is not admirable—if there is anything shoddy or unworthy of praise— do not think about these things."[12]

As a Jewish psychiatrist who spent three grim years in a Nazi prison camp, Viktor Frankl lived each hour with the realization that he might be among those who would be exterminated that day. Many who were interned with Frankl died from worrying about their death. Frankl chose not to do that. He developed a positive outlook that enabled him to peer through the broken slats in the wall of his cold hut and take pleasure in the beauty of a sunset. He developed a sense of humor so that he could laugh even in the midst of his pain. He found meaning in his suffering, and he tried to help others find that meaning also. As he reflected back upon his prison experience, he wrote:

The experiences of camp life show that man does have a choice of action. There were enough examples, often of a heroic nature, which proved that apathy could be overcome, irritability suppressed. Man *can* preserve a vestige of spiritual freedom, of independence of mind, even in such terrible conditions of psychic and physical stress.... Everything can be taken from a man but one thing: the last of the human freedoms—to choose one's attitude in any given set of circumstances, to choose one's own way. And there were always choices to make. Every day, every hour, offered the opportunity to make a decision.... In the final analysis it becomes clear that the sort of person the prisoner became was the result of an inner decision, and not the result of camp influences alone. Fundamentally, therefore, any man can, even under such circumstances, decide what shall become of him—mentally and spiritually.[13]

The word of God confirms the truth of Frankl's words. We do have a choice to make about our thinking. We are expected to make the correct decision. The prophet Isaiah wrote, "You will keep him in perfect peace, whose mind is stayed on You, because he trusts in You" (26:3). Paul instructed the Corinthians that they were to bring "every thought into captivity to the obedience of Christ" (2 Cor. 10:5).

TO AVOID ANXIETY WE MUST DO THE PROPER THINGS

There once was a highway sign in Canada that read, "Take care which rut you choose. You will be in it for the next twenty-five miles." Our thoughts make the ruts that our actions will have to follow. Our thinking issues in our doing. What we ponder we end up practicing. Our learning determines our living.

The Philippian believers were instructed to practice the things they had heard, seen, learned, and received from Paul. The items on that action list included the following:

- Loving more (1:9)
- Having greater discernment (1:9–10)
- Being sincere and without offense (1:10)
- Being filled with the fruits of righteousness (1:11)
- Having conduct worthy of the gospel (1:27)
- Standing fast in one spirit (1:27)
- Striving together for the gospel (1:27)
- Being like-minded, of one accord (2:2)
- Esteeming others better than themselves (2:3)
- Working out their own salvation in fear and trembling (2:12)
- Doing all things without complaining and disputing (2:14)
- Holding fast the word of life (2:16)
- Looking out for false teachers (3:1–3)

When Paul spoke of the things learned and received, he was talking about careful exhortation. When he spoke of those things heard and seen, he was referring to concrete example. Paul was a living example of the conduct he expected from them.

There was once a preacher of whom it was said, "He preached so well in the pulpit that it was a tragedy for him ever to go out of it, but he lived so poorly that it was unfortunate that he ever entered it." Paul was the exact opposite of this.

Dealing with anxiety, then, is a matter of proper thinking and proper action. When we follow through on Paul's advice, there is a promise of peace for each one.

THE PROMISE: PEACE
GOD'S PROTECTION

The peace of God acts as a guard or sentinel at the door of the heart and mind to provide security. The word the apostle used is *garrison*. Paul was promising that when we pray and think and do as God has instructed, then His peace becomes the guard that is stationed at the door of our hearts and minds. This peace-guard keeps anxiety away from us. It is this guarding of the heart and mind that provides the Christian with a decided edge when it comes to dealing with the pressures of the day.

Dr. S. I. McMillen and Dr. David E. Stern wrote a book about diseases that we suffer because we refuse to follow God's instruction given to us in the Bible. In the book *None of These Diseases* they tell this story about a rather famous worrier:

> In 1929, business tycoon J. C. Penney was hospi-
> talized because of his severe anxiety. One night he
> was sure he was going to die so he wrote farewell
> letters to his wife and son. But he survived the

night, and hearing singing the next morning in the chapel felt drawn to go in. A group was singing, "God Will Take Care of You," after which followed Bible reading and prayer.

Penney said, "Suddenly something happened. I can't explain it. It was a miracle. I felt as if I had been instantly lifted out of the darkness of a dungeon into warm brilliant sunlight. I felt as if I had been transported from hell to paradise. I felt the power of God as I had never felt it before.

"I realized then that I alone was responsible for all my troubles. I knew that God with His love was there to help me. From that day to this, my life has been free from worry. The most dramatic and glorious minutes of my life were those I spent in that chapel that morning."[14]

GOD'S PRESENCE

Philippians 4:9 tells us that not only will we have *the peace of God* but, even better, we will be protected by *the God of peace*. He will be with us, and His presence will be our comfort and encouragement when difficult problems assail our minds.

GOD'S PEACE

The peace we gain will go beyond the understanding of the average man. It will pass all understanding. Our peace will be supernatural. J. J. Müller explains the surpassing nature of this peace:

It probably means that the peace which God gives excels and surpasses all our own intellectual calculations and considerations, all our contemplations and premeditated ideas of how to get rid of our cares.... What God gives surpasses all that we ask or think (Eph. 3:20).[15]

It is the peace that Jesus promised to His followers:

Peace I leave with you, My peace I give to you; not as the world gives do I give to you. Let not your heart be troubled, neither let it be afraid. (John 14:27)

These things I have spoken to you, that in Me you may have peace. In the world you will have tribulation; but be of good cheer, I have overcome the world. (John 16:33)

Norman Harrison's comments on this passage in John 16 provide a good summary of all we have discussed in this chapter:

Note the contrasting experience: "In Me ... peace. In the world ... tribulation." Jesus gives us peace. The world gives us worry. Which is to prevail? And what is to decide the issue? How fully Jesus understood, and how faithfully He characterized

the world in which we move. It is a world of worry
and vexation of spirit.... The hope of escape is in
Jesus' reassuring words: "Be of good cheer; I have
overcome the world." The victory is already won
for those of us who are "in Him." The secret lies in
our power so to appropriate that victory as to make
it, potentially and practically, our very own.[16]

So when the *problem* is worry, the *prescription* is prayer. When
prayer has cleansed the mind from the anxious thoughts, the *program* is to think and do those things that are commanded of us in
God's Word. The *promise* for all who follow this counsel is peace ...
the peace of God and, best of all, the God of peace.

Years ago, in the pioneer days of aviation, a pilot
was making a flight around the world. After he
was two hours out of his last landing field, he
heard a noise in his plane, which he recognized
as the gnawing of a rat. He realized that while his
plane had been on the ground a rat had gotten in.
For all he knew the rat could be gnawing through
a vital cable or control of the plane.

It was a very serious situation. He was both
concerned and anxious. At first he did not
know what to do. It was two hours back to the
landing field from which he had taken off and
more than two hours to the next field ahead.

Then he remembered that the rat is a rodent. It is not made for heights; it is made to live on the ground and under the ground. Therefore the pilot began to climb. He went up a thousand feet, then another thousand and another until he was more than twenty thousand feet up. The gnawing ceased. The rat was dead. He could not survive in the atmosphere of those heights. More than two hours later the pilot brought the plane safely to the next landing field and found the dead rat.

Worry is a rodent. It cannot live in the secret place of the Most High. It cannot breathe in the atmosphere made vital through prayer and familiarity with the Scripture. Worry dies when we ascend to the Lord through prayer and His Word.[17]

But I rejoiced in the Lord greatly that now at last your care for me has flourished again; though you surely did care, but you lacked opportunity. Not that I speak in regard to need, for I have learned in whatever state I am, to be content: I know how to be abased, and I know how to abound. Everywhere and in all things I have learned both to be full and to be hungry, both to abound and to suffer need. I can do all things through Christ who strengthens me.

Nevertheless you have done well that you shared in my distress. Now you Philippians know also that in the beginning of the gospel, when I departed from Macedonia, no church shared with me concerning giving and receiving but you only. For even in Thessalonica you sent aid once and again for my necessities. Not that I seek the gift, but I seek the fruit that abounds to your account. Indeed I have all and abound. I am full, having received from Epaphroditus the things sent from you, a sweet-smelling aroma, an acceptable sacrifice, well pleasing to God. And my God shall supply all your need according to His riches in glory by Christ Jesus. Now to our God and Father be glory forever and ever. Amen.

Greet every saint in Christ Jesus. The brethren who are with me greet you. All the saints greet you, but especially those who are of Caesar's household.

The grace of our Lord Jesus Christ be with you all. Amen.

Philippians 4:10–23

THE JOY OF SERENITY

Philippians 4:10–23

*And my God shall supply all your need according
to His riches in glory by Christ Jesus.*

More. If there's a single word that summarizes
American hopes and obsessions, that's it. More
money. More success. More luxuries and gizmos.
We live for more—for our next raise, our next
house; and the things we already have, however
wonderful they are, tend to pale in comparison
with the things we might still get.[1]

These are the words of Laurence Shames in his book *The
Hunger for More*. In this analysis of contemporary values, Shames
traces discontent to the ravaging appetite of a nation gone mad
after prosperity:

During the past decade, many people came to believe there didn't have to be a purpose. The mechanism didn't require it. Consumption kept the workers working, which kept the paychecks coming, which kept the people spending, which kept inventors inventing and investors investing, which meant there was more to consume. The system, properly understood, was independent of values and needed no philosophy to prop it up. It was a perfect circle, complete in itself—and empty in the middle.[2]

As he wrestled with the significance of this problem, Shames looked at the empty circle:

It is my conviction that the version of success that was dominant in America in the 1980s—a success defined almost exclusively in terms of money and virtually without reference to the substance of one's achievement—has served us badly.... A vision of success based on money alone—more money each year—is a dangerous dead end at a historical moment when real wealth can no longer be counted on to increase. Over time, by the rigid rules of that game, there will inevitably be more losers, fewer winners, less joy, and more desperation in the contest. For reasons of simple self-interest, we need to cultivate a new definition of the well-lived life.[3]

In his book *Simple Faith*, Charles Swindoll cites a poem that expresses the discontent so prevalent in our society.

It was spring
But it was summer I wanted,
The warm days,
And the great outdoors.

It was summer,
But it was fall I wanted,
The colorful leaves,
And the cool, dry air.

It was fall,
But it was winter I wanted,
The beautiful snow,
And the joy of the holiday season.

It was winter,
But it was spring I wanted,
The warmth
And the blossoming of nature.

I was a child,
But it was adulthood I wanted.
The freedom,
And the respect.

I was 20,
But it was 30 I wanted,
To be mature,
And sophisticated.

I was middle-aged,
But it was 20 I wanted,
The youth,
And the free spirit.

I was retired,
But it was middle age I wanted,
The presence of mind,
Without limitations.

My life was over.
But I never got what I wanted.[4]

I have met so many people about whom this poem could have been written. They are always searching for contentment but never finding it. They are always unhappy in the hunt and almost always affecting someone with gloom and dreariness along the way.

Harold Kushner tells a humorous story that expresses the confusion that reigns as man searches for contentment:

> I heard this story about a bright young man, a pre-med sophomore at Stanford University. To reward him for having done so well in school, his parents gave him a trip to the Far East for the summer vacation between his sophomore and junior years. While there he met a guru who said to him, "Don't you see how you are poisoning your soul with this success-oriented way of life? Your idea of happiness is to stay up all night studying for an exam so you can get a better grade than your best friend. Your idea of a good marriage is not to find the woman who will make you whole, but to win the girl that everyone else wants. That's not how people are supposed to live. Give it up; come join us in an atmosphere where we all share and love each other." The young man had completed four years at a competitive high school to get into Stanford, plus two years of pre-med courses at the university. He was ripe for this sort of approach. He called his parents from Tokyo and told them he would not be coming home. He was dropping out of school to live in an ashram.

Six months later, his parents got a letter from him: "Dear Mom and Dad, I know you weren't happy with the decision I made last summer, but I want to tell you how happy it has made me. For the first time in my life, I am at peace. Here there is no competing, no hustling, no trying to get ahead of anyone else. Here we are all equal, and we all share. This way of life is so much in harmony with the inner essence of my soul that in only six months I've become the number two disciple in the entire ashram, and I think I can be number one by June!"[5]

The quest for peace of mind and contentment can be an elusive journey. As we turn our attention to this last section of Philippians, we have already learned about the "peace of God, which surpasses all understanding" (4:7) and the God of peace who promises to be with us (v. 9). We have discovered that these blessings can be ours as we learn right praying (v. 6), right thinking (v. 8), and right living (v. 9).

After Paul voiced his gratitude for the Philippians' continued care for him, he expressed his own spirit of contentment. He was not rejoicing simply because they had sent him a gift, nor was he hinting that he would like another one. He was going on record as being content, whether they supported him or not. He said, "I have learned … to be content" (v. 11).

The word *content* literally means "self-sufficient"; a man should be sufficient to himself in all things.

> The Stoics made a good deal out of the virtue of self-sufficiency or independence of external circumstances. They held that a man should be sufficient in and unto himself in all things. When asked who was the wealthiest, Socrates said, "He who is content with least, for self-sufficiency is nature's wealth."
>
> But, though Paul uses the Stoic word, he has more than the Stoic idea. He expressly disclaims this mere self-sufficiency: "Not that we are sufficient of ourselves, to account anything as from ourselves; but our sufficiency is from God."[6]

In the New Testament, the Greek word for "contentment" is also translated "satisfied," "adequate," "competent," or "sufficient." It is the word used in 2 Corinthians 12:9 when God told Paul, "My grace is sufficient for you." Charles Kelley defined contentment this way: "Christian contentment is the God-given ability to be satisfied with the loving provision of God in any and every situation."[7]

For the Christian, contentment is both an independent and a dependent quality. The things the world says are necessary for contentment do not matter to the Christian. The things the world says are unimportant are of vital importance if the Christian is to be content.

CONTENTMENT—IN THE PLACE WHERE GOD HAS STATIONED YOU

Paul's contentment was something he possessed "in whatever state" he was in and "in all things." In Philippians 4:12, he said he had learned how to be content when he was *in* poverty, but he did not say he was content *with* poverty. He said he was content when he was abased or suffering need.

Paul was certainly qualified to make such a judgment. He had once been stoned and dragged out of a city (Acts 14:19). He had been beaten and thrown into jail (16:22–24). He had been plotted against by the Jews (20:3). He had been "in tribulations, in needs, in distresses, in stripes, in imprisonments, in tumults, in labors, in sleeplessness, in fastings" (2 Cor. 6:4–5). He had experienced trouble on every side, accompanied by outward conflicts and inward fears (7:5).

He had known abundant labors, frequent imprisonments, and close encounters with death. Five times he had received thirty-nine stripes from the Jews. Three times he was beaten with rods. Once he was stoned and three times he experienced shipwreck. He once spent a night and a day in the water. He had faced death from robbers, from his own countrymen, from the Gentiles, and from false brethren. He had often experienced weariness, sleeplessness, hunger, thirst, fastings, cold, and nakedness (11:23–27). In the midst of all these things Paul had *learned* how to be content.

It might seem easier to find contentment in times of abundance than in times of stress. There are many who would not agree! Thomas Carlyle would be among them. He said, "Adversity is sometimes hard upon a man, but for one man who can stand prosperity, there are a hundred that will stand adversity."[8]

Years ago, a syndicated column carried the story of a group of famous American financiers who in the early 1920s had met at the Edgewater Beach Hotel in Chicago. In personal wealth and financial bearings, they controlled more money than was in the national treasury. From time to time, their names appeared in the press; their influence was enormous, their success fabulous.

Twenty-five years later the writer of the column called the roll of these princes of the financial world. One of them, a man who had cornered millions through wheat speculation, had died abroad, insolvent. Another, the president of the nation's largest independent steel company, had died broke. The president of the New York Stock Exchange had recently been released from prison. A member of the cabinet in the Harding administration, after being let out of prison for health reasons, had died at home. The greatest exploiter of the bear market in Wall Street had committed suicide. The leader of the world's greatest monopoly had also died at his own hand. In summarizing the list of men, the columnist said, "All of these men had learned how to make big money, but not one of them had learned how to live."[9]

Paul knew how to live in good times as well as in bad. In Philippians 4:12 he used the word *abound* twice as he described his contentment in times of plenty. Abound means "more than enough." It is probable that Paul grew up in a moderately affluent home, and even after his conversion he had experienced God's abundant provision for his needs. When they were starting the church at Philippi, Paul and his associates were entertained at the home of Lydia, who was a prominent wealthy woman (Acts 16:15, 40). Paul and Silas were given a banquet at the home of the Philippian jailer (16:33–34). Paul was entertained by the natives on the island of Malta after he had survived a shipwreck (28:2). The whole story of the Philippians' relationship with Paul was one of caring and giving and ministering.

But for Paul it really didn't matter. Whether he was feasting or fasting, rich or poor, he had learned how to be content. When writing to his young disciple, Paul instructed Timothy in this doctrine:

> Now godliness with contentment is great gain. For we brought nothing into this world, and it is certain we can carry nothing out. And having food and clothing, with these we shall be content. But those who desire to be rich fall into temptation and a snare, and into many foolish and harmful lusts which drown men in destruction and perdition. For the love of money is a root of all kinds of evil, for which some have strayed from the faith in their greediness, and pierced themselves through with many sorrows. (1 Tim. 6:6–10)

Someone once explained to me that Philippians 4:11–12 qualifies four basic things for the believer to be concerned about:

- What I put on—clothes
- What I put in—food
- What I put up—a house to live in
- What I put away—money for the future

Paul's contentment was inclusive of any situation and any location. He had learned to be content "everywhere and in all things." May I remind you that Paul was not writing this from a penthouse or a cruise ship but from jail.

In the second half of verse 12 there is a Greek verb that means, "I have learned the secret." Alec Motyer explains what that expression would have meant to those who read it:

> This was used in the Greek mystery religions to describe people who had worked their way up through the various lower "degrees" and had finally been admitted into full possession of the "mystery" itself. Paul is saying, "I have made my way up through the degrees of progressive detachment from the things of the world, its comforts and its discomforts alike, and finally I have reached maturity on this point. I know the secret; circumstances can never again touch me." … Paul had learned the lesson. Bit by bit, test by test, circumstance by circumstance, he persevered through the lower degrees until he finally "graduated" and the "secret" was his.

Contentment did not come easily. He purchased
it at the price of exacting discipline.[10]

So many people go through life thinking that if they could just
relocate, they would be content. If they could just go to another
church, they would be content. If they could just get a job in
another community, they would be content.

A man once came to Socrates and asked him about the unhappiness of one of his friends. Socrates answered, "The trouble with
that man is that he takes himself with him wherever he goes."

CONTENTMENT—BECAUSE
OF THE POWER OF GOD THAT
STRENGTHENS YOU

When, in verse 13, the apostle confidently wrote that he could
do all things through Christ who strengthened him, he was
simply saying he was continually energized in all things by the
strengthening of Christ. He was not talking about an outward
set of circumstances but an inward source of strength. This is not
contentment in a place, but in a Person. James S. Stewart explains
what this verse means:

> Christ is the redeemed man's new environment.
> The human body, by the acts of eating and drink-
> ing and breathing, is continually drawing for its
> strength upon the resources of its physical envi-
> ronment. So the Christian spirit, by prayer and

worship and surrender, makes contact and keeps contact with its spiritual environment, which is Christ: thus the soul draws for its strength upon the supplies of power which in Christ are quite inexhaustible.[11]

This quiet strength enables a believer to live in the place where God has put him and be content.

CONTENTMENT—BECAUSE OF THE PEOPLE OF GOD WHO SUPPORT YOU

Paul's main purpose for writing this letter was to express his gratitude for the gift that had been sent to him from the Philippian congregation. He began this section by telling of his own joy at receiving their gift. While he noted the interruption that had occurred in their care for him, he was not scolding them. He knew they had tried to minister to him but were unable. William Hendriksen suggests two possible reasons for their inability to assist Paul: "It may have been that no messenger had been immediately available, or that for some reason or other it had been impossible to collect the gift from the various members."[12]

The gift that arrived was sent by way of Epaphroditus. Paul confirmed that in verse 18: "Indeed I have all and abound. I am full, having received from Epaphroditus the things sent from you, a sweet-smelling aroma, an acceptable sacrifice, well pleasing to God."

As Paul evaluated the generosity of the Philippians, he came to three important conclusions concerning giving and receiving:

- Giving brings blessing to the one who receives the gift. Paul was very thankful for their generous gift. Because they gave, he said, "I have all and abound. I am full" (v. 18).
- Giving brings blessing to God. From God's perspective, the Philippian gift was "a sweet-smelling aroma, an acceptable sacrifice, well pleasing to God" (v. 18).
- Giving brings blessing to the one who gives the gift. Paul told the Philippians they had "done well" (v. 14), and he described their gift as "fruit that abounds to your account" (v. 17).

This is a proper motive for Christians to cultivate: they should seek out opportunities to expend their generosity upon the needy, because by selling what they have and giving alms they would make for themselves "purses that do not grow old ... a treasure in the heavens that does not fail" (Luke 12:33). For God would not be unrighteous and forget their work and the love which they showed him when they ministered to the saints (Heb. 6:10).[13]

In the last verses of this chapter, Paul mentioned three groups of people who had been used by God to support and sustain him during his days of confinement in Rome. The first group was "the brethren who are with me." It is of great value to observe how often the apostle spoke of being with others in the ministry. He was not afraid of being alone, but he seldom was unaccompanied. Here is one scholar's attempt at identifying these brethren:

> His youthful disciple and associate Timotheus ... seems to have been with him during ... nearly the whole of his captivity.... Luke, "the beloved physician" now his fellow-laborer and perhaps his medical attendant, hereafter his biographer, is constantly by his side.... Philippi dispatches Epaphroditus.... Aristarchus is present from Thessalonica.... Delegates from the Asiatic churches too were with him: Tychicus, a native of the Roman province of Asia ... the Apostle's companion both in earlier and later days, and Epaphras the evangelist of ... Colossae.[14]

Second, Paul spoke of "all the saints." There are many who believe these were the "saints" listed by name in Romans 16. Among them were Amplias, Apelles, Stachys, Rufus, Hermes, Tryphena, and Tryphosa.

The third party included "those who are of Caesar's household." This description embraced a vast number of people from all over the empire. It would have included household slaves, soldiers, senators, knights, men and women of wealth and status, and many others who were drawn to Rome because it was the control center for the sprawling kingdom. Many of these men and women had been won to Christ by the testimony of Paul, who earlier in his letter had described his imprisonment as that which had "turned out for the furtherance of the gospel" (Phil. 1:12).

Looking over the entire scene, it is amazing to see how God met His apostle's needs through a support system in Philippi and a support system in Rome. Paul's serenity was the result of this support from the people of God.

CONTENTMENT—WHEN THE PROMISE OF GOD SUSTAINS YOU

Paul reminded the Philippians that the God who had cared for *his* needs through their loving concern would also care for *their* needs as they trusted Him! This promise is often taken out of context. It was given to encourage those who were sacrificial in their response to the needs of God's work. There is another promise very similar to this one that is also found in the middle of some strong teaching on stewardship: "And God is able to make all grace abound toward you, that you, always having all sufficiency in all things, may have an abundance for every good work" (2 Cor. 9:8).

Paul had been rejoicing in the fact that the Philippians had supplied his need. Now he told them that God would supply their need. His promise to them was *personal*: "my God." It was *positive*: "shall supply." It was *pointed*: "all your need." It was *plentiful*: "according to His riches in glory," and it was *powerful*: "by Christ Jesus."

This is a consistent principle in the working of God with men. "Give, and it will be given to you: good measure, pressed down, shaken together, and running over will be put into your bosom. For with the same measure that you use, it will be measured back to you" (Luke 6:38).

> Lend your boat for a whole afternoon to Christ that it may be His floating pulpit, and He will return it to you laden with fish. Place your upper room at His disposal for a single meal and He will fill it and the whole house with the Holy Spirit of Pentecost. Place in His hands your barley loaves and fish, and He will not only satisfy your hunger, but add twelve baskets full of fragments. The Philippians sent three or four presents to a suffering and much needing servant of God, and from that moment … every need of theirs would be supplied…. We scratch the surface of the soil and insert our few little seeds, and within a few months the acreage is covered by a prolific harvest in which a hundredfold is given for every grain which we seemed to throw away. God refuses to be in debt to any man.[15]

One of my favorite professors in seminary was a quiet and wonderful man by the name of John Witmer. On one occasion as he was describing his growing-up days during the Depression, he told this story:

> During the Great Depression, the bank in which my father was an officer was forced to close. I was convinced my father would be out of work. Though I was only twelve, I knew I had to get a job to help support the family. A nearby corner grocer hired me after school and Saturdays for a dollar a week to sweep the floors and deliver groceries.
>
> When I told my father, he replied, "I appreciate your concern and desire to help, son, but I am trusting the Lord to meet our needs. We belong to Him and He will take care of His own."
>
> God honored my father's faith. He never went a day without employment through the entire Depression.[16]

Contentment can be ours in *the place where God has stationed us*. It is always the result of *the power of God that strengthens us*. It is usually bolstered by *the people of God who support us*, and it is guaranteed by *the promise of God that sustains us*.

A bishop of the early church, who was a remarkable example of the virtue of contentment, was asked his secret. The venerable old man replied:

It consists in nothing more than making a right use of my eyes. In whatever state I am, I first of all look up to heaven and remember that my principal business here is to get there.

Then I look down upon the earth, and call to mind how small a place I shall occupy in it when I die and am buried. I then look around in the world, and observe what multitudes there are who are in many respects more unhappy than myself. Thus I learn where true happiness is placed, where all our cares must end, and what little reason I have to complain.[17]

READERS' GUIDE

For Personal Reflection and Group Study

Before beginning your personal or group study of *Count It All Joy*, take time to read these introductory comments.

If you are working through the study on your own, you may want to adapt certain sections (for example, the icebreakers) and record your responses to all questions in a separate notebook. You might find it more enriching or motivating to study with a partner with whom you can share answers or insights.

If you are leading a group, you may want to ask your group members to read each assigned chapter and work through the study questions before the group meets. This isn't always easy for busy adults, so encourage them with occasional phone calls or notes between meetings. Help members manage their time by pointing out how they can cover a few pages each day. Also have them identify a regular time of the day or week that they can devote to the study. They too may write their responses to the questions in notebooks.

Notice that each session includes the following features:

- Session Topic—a brief statement summarizing the session
- Icebreakers—activities to help group members get better acquainted with the session topic and/or with each other
- Group Discovery Questions—a list of questions to encourage individual discovery or group participation
- Personal Application Questions—an aid to applying the knowledge gained through study to one's personal living. (Note: These are important questions for group members to answer for themselves even if they do not wish to discuss their responses in the meeting.)
- Optional Activities—supplemental ideas that will enhance the study
- Prayer Focus—suggestions for turning one's learning into prayer
- Assignment—activities or preparation to complete prior to the next session

Here are a few tips that can help you more effectively lead small-group studies:

- Pray for each group member, asking the Lord to help you create an open atmosphere where everyone will feel free to share with one another and you.

- Encourage group members to bring their Bibles, as well as their texts, to each session. This study is based on the *New King James Version*, but it is good to have several translations on hand for purposes of comparison.

- Start and end on time. This is especially important for the first meeting, because it will set the pattern for the rest of the sessions.

- Begin with prayer, asking the Holy Spirit to open hearts and minds and to give understanding so that truth will be applied.

- Involve everyone. As learners, we retain only 10 percent of what we hear, 20 percent of what we see, 65 percent of what we hear and see, but 90 percent of what we hear, see, and do.

- Promote a relaxed environment. Arrange the chairs in a circle or semicircle. This allows eye contact among members and encourages dynamic discussion. Be relaxed in your own attitude and manner. Be willing to share, yourself.

1 THE JOY OF COMMUNITY
PHILIPPIANS 1:1–11
SESSION TOPIC

The Christian life is a life lived in community, characterized by joy, with love as its highest goal.

ICEBREAKERS (CHOOSE ONE)

1. Break into groups of two. Interview your partner, and allow your partner to interview you. Take turns introducing your partner to the whole group.

2. The author speaks of the essential nature of community and fellowship to the Christian believer. Name one or more of the communities to which you belong (e.g., family, church, neighborhood, job, interest groups) and tell how this community is important to you.

GROUP DISCOVERY QUESTIONS

1. Why is fellowship necessary? What happens when we lack fellowship?

2. The author quotes Amy Carmichael on "unlove" and its deadly, spreading power. Have you ever witnessed the spread of "unlove" through a community? Describe this occurrence and its effect.

3. In the greeting of Paul's letter to the Philippians, what is the significance of the words *grace* and *peace* being used together and in that order?

4. The author speaks of the diversity found in the Philippian church. Is your church community homogeneous or diverse? Why?

5. According to the author, love is useless unless it is expressed. How did Paul express his love for the Philippians? How can a spirit of gratitude be an expression of love?

6. Why was Paul so sure of the love the Philippians had for him? According to C. S. Lewis, what is the secret to loving someone?

7. In verses 9–11, Paul prayed for the growth and maturity of his Philippian friends. For what specifically did he pray? Express this prayer in your own words.

PERSONAL APPLICATION QUESTIONS

1. What have been the benefits of fellowship in your own life? Are you lacking in fellowship? If so, talk to others in the group or to your pastor about where you could receive fellowship. If you're not but you know someone who is, how could you help him or her?

2. Humble service is an important theme in Philippians. What is your definition of healthy humility? Who in your life best exemplifies this trait? Is humble service a characteristic of your own life?

3. How unified is your community? What can you do to help build unity in your community?

4. Paul called the Philippians to unity within diversity. How tolerant are you of diversity within your community?

5. Think of someone you love. What is one way you can express your love to him or her this week? (Remember that what makes you feel loved is not necessarily what makes someone else feel loved.)

6. In your closest relationship, how difficult is it to always seek the best interest of the one you love?

OPTIONAL ACTIVITIES

1. Express your love to someone in your community this week through an act of hospitality. (For example, invite someone to your home for dinner.)

2. Make a prayer box. You will need three-by-five index cards and a file box with seven dividers. At the top of each card, write the name of a person in your community for whom you would like to pray. Under the name write specific things you want to pray for that person. Divide the cards into seven groups and file each group under a different day of the week. Use your prayer box during your devotional time to pray for the people filed under that specific day. In the front of your box, make a card for yourself and anyone else you want to pray for daily.

PRAYER FOCUS

Use Paul's prayer for the Philippians (vv. 9–11) to pray for your community.

ASSIGNMENT

1. If you do not already keep a journal, begin one now. This week, reflect on the importance of your community in your life.

2. Read chapter 2 of the text and work through the corresponding study.

2 THE JOY OF ADVERSITY
PHILIPPIANS 1:12–26
SESSION TOPIC

Good things can come from adversity.

ICEBREAKERS (CHOOSE ONE)

1. Tell about a time in your life or the life of someone close to you when good came from adversity.

2. Give some examples of well-known people through whom God used adversity to further His purpose.

GROUP DISCOVERY QUESTIONS

1. What were some of the positive results of Paul's imprisonment?

2. What did Paul mean by "For to me, to live is Christ, and to die is gain"?

3. Can good results ever come from evil motives? What was Paul talking about in verses 15–18?

4. Do you believe it is God who brings adversity into our lives? Why or why not?

5. Dr. Jeremiah points out that adversity makes some people better and others bitter. What makes the difference?

6. What are the seven advantages to adversity? Give an example of each of these seven principles from the Bible, from the life of a well-known Christian, or from your own experience.

7. What were some of the adversities Paul faced during his ministry (Acts 20:6–28:31; 2 Cor. 11:23–27)? How was he able to keep a positive attitude?

PERSONAL APPLICATION QUESTIONS

1. Think of an adverse situation from your own life. Can you see any of the seven principles at work?

2. What is the most common way for you to respond to adversity? What can you learn from Paul?

3. What was Paul's attitude toward death? How is it the same or different from your own attitude?

4. When people are in a life-and-death crisis like Paul, they are sometimes better able to focus on what is really important. What was Paul's focus? Where is your focus? With all of life's demands, how do you sort out what is really important?

5. Give an example from your own experience where courage was contagious. From whom do you draw courage? Who draws courage from you?

6. What have been some of the major adversities you have faced? Are you stronger for having faced them? If so, in what ways?

7. Has learning about the advantages of adversity been an encouragement to you in whatever trouble you are facing? If so, how have you been encouraged? How could you encourage someone else?

OPTIONAL ACTIVITIES

1. Get out the prayer box you made last week. Under each name write down the adversities currently being faced by that person and pray specifically for those struggles.

2. In your journal, write down an adversity you are currently facing. Envision how you would like to respond to this adversity and write this response down.

3. If you do not already have a support person or group, seek out someone with whom you can share adversities and encouragement.

PRAYER FOCUS

Pray for others and yourself in the struggles you are currently facing. Pray that God will help you keep a clear conscience, a courageous testimony, and a Christ-centered focus.

ASSIGNMENT

1. This week include in your journal the adversities you face each day and how you are able to face them.

2. Read chapter 3 of the text and work through the corresponding study.

3 THE JOY OF INTEGRITY
PHILIPPIANS 1:27–30
SESSION TOPIC

Our lives must be guided by four priorities—conduct, consistency, cooperation, and courage—if we are to claim victory over the principalities and powers of this world.

ICEBREAKERS (CHOOSE ONE)

1. Imagine you are a Christian in Paul's Philippian church. The authorities have been questioning some of your friends and have accused them of disloyalty to Rome. How would you explain to the Roman authorities what it means to be a follower of Jesus?

2. The author quotes Charles Colson's description of an antidraft poster that read, "Nothing is worth dying for." What would you die for?

GROUP DISCOVERY QUESTIONS

1. The word *politeuomai*, translated "conversation" in the KJV, speaks of the conduct expected of a citizen. What are the privileges and responsibilities of citizenship in this country?

2. What are the responsibilities incumbent on citizens of the kingdom of God?

3. Many of the early church leaders described the Christian's life as that of a sojourner (a foreigner residing in or traveling through another country). What opportunities do Christians encounter as we "sojourn" in this country? What challenges and/or dangers do we face as foreigners in a strange land?

4. The author suggests that the story of Daniel is a great illustration of a consistent lifestyle. How do you imagine Daniel was able to live such a life under these difficult circumstances?

5. Certainly one of the keys to Daniel's great strength was his strong sense of personal identity. His identity was rooted in the history and traditions of Israel. "Now when Daniel knew that the writing was signed, he went home. And in his upper room, with his windows open toward Jerusalem, he knelt down on his knees

three times that day, and prayed and gave thanks before his God, as was his custom since early days" (Dan. 6:10). What traditions (practices or disciplines) do we as Christians observe to remind us of who we are?

6. The author, quoting Warren Wiersbe, states that the church must "face up to her sins, repent, and start being the true church of that Gospel. We Christians boast that we are not ashamed of the Gospel of Christ, but perhaps the Gospel of Christ is ashamed of us." In what ways has the church's ministry failed to match its message?

7. In what areas have you seen your church community successfully "striving together"? Where could your community's ministry be strengthened by attending to our common struggle?

PERSONAL APPLICATION QUESTIONS

1. The author quotes Sheldon Vanauken, who states that "the best argument for Christianity is Christians: their joy, their certainty, their completeness." Do these attributes characterize your life? If not, what are the struggles that you face in trying to live such a life?

2. Jesus said, "Blessed are you when they revile and persecute you" (Matt. 5:11). Yet most of us today are not explicitly reviled, and rarely do we face anything that could be considered persecution. Why do we seem to encounter so little opposition today? Are there other, more subtle, forms of opposition that confront us today? What are they?

3. What attributes of Paul's life would you like to see in yourself?

4. What are some of the important events from Paul's life that contributed to his psychological and spiritual formation? How did Paul respond to these events?

5. One common aspect of great leaders throughout the history of the church is the use of a spiritual discipline or rule. What are some disciplines you would like to incorporate into your life? (You're already following a rule if you've been using your prayer box and keeping a journal from week to week.)

6. Another important aspect of Paul's life is that he cultivated close relationships with Christians wherever he traveled. Choose one or two close friends with whom you can share your struggles and victories. Ask them to help you be accountable in following your spiritual rule.

OPTIONAL ACTIVITIES

1. Read some of the writings of the early church fathers. Most of these works are filled with extraordinary examples of Christians striving together in difficult circumstances. For starters, try the *Epistle of Polycarp to the Philippians*, the *Martyrdom of Polycarp*, or the letters of Ignatius. There are numerous translations of these works available through your local bookstore.

2. Select the card with your name from your prayer box. Write down the disciplines you wish to incorporate into your spiritual

rule. (Remember to start with a very simple rule.) For now, your rule might consist only of your prayer box and your journal. Try to follow your rule for several weeks (or months) before adding anything to it. Aim for simplicity and consistency, not volume.

PRAYER FOCUS

Pray for God's help and wisdom as you select and begin to follow a spiritual rule.

ASSIGNMENT

1. In your journal reflect on the stories of Daniel and Paul and the characteristics that made their lives remarkable.

2. Read chapter 4 of the text and work through the corresponding study.

4 THE JOY OF UNITY
PHILIPPIANS 2:1–11
SESSION TOPIC

We are to come together in Christian unity, having the servant attitude of Christ.

ICEBREAKERS (CHOOSE ONE)

1. Give some examples from movies or television of how our culture encourages a fixation with self.

2. Name someone you know who exhibits a servant attitude.

GROUP DISCOVERY QUESTIONS

1. What did Paul mean when he said, "Let this mind be in you which was also in Christ Jesus" (v. 5)?

2. What is the price we must pay for unity? How does the story of the cross give us a glimpse of this price?

3. How is the Incarnation a demonstration of humility?

4. In what way did Christ empty Himself?

5. For what purpose did Christ come in the flesh?

6. Why is an attitude of humble service essential to unity in the body?

7. According to the author, "There is no spiritual unity without doctrinal oneness." Do you agree? If so, what do you consider to be the core doctrines essential to unity? Can you have unity with people from Christian denominations other than your own?

8. Give some examples (other than from movies and television) of how our culture is at odds with Paul's injunction to lose the self. How can we foster selflessness in ourselves and our children?

PERSONAL APPLICATION QUESTIONS

1. In what ways do you have an attitude of humble service? In what ways do you not have a servant attitude?

2. What makes having a servant attitude most difficult for you? What can you do to encourage the development of the mind of Christ in yourself?

3. Paul probably wrote Philippians 2:1–11 to deal with the friction that had developed in the Philippian church. Is it possible to have a church without friction? Why or why not?

4. In relationships, how comfortable are you with conflict? Are you more likely to try to resolve conflict or ignore the fact that conflict exists? What do you think usually happens when conflict is ignored?

5. According to the author, the word *comfort* in verse 1 indicates a spoken word of encouragement. When has a word of encouragement been most meaningful to you? Is there someone who needs your encouragement?

6. The word *each* in verse 3 is a reminder that we have a personal responsibility for the unity of the body. What can you do to encourage unity in your church community?

OPTIONAL ACTIVITIES

1. Find verses from Paul's letters that show Paul's lowliness of mind.

2. Look through the names of the people in your prayer box. Are you involved in a conflict with any of these people? If so, what can you do to help resolve this conflict?

PRAYER FOCUS

Pray for the unity of your congregation, your denomination, and the church around the world. Ask God for faithfulness in building unity in your congregation.

ASSIGNMENT

1. In your journal this week, write down any interpersonal conflicts you have and how they are resolved.

2. Read chapter 5 of the text and work through the corresponding study.

5 THE JOY OF RESPONSIBILITY
PHILIPPIANS 2:12–16
SESSION TOPIC

Be responsible to discipline your own moral character.

ICEBREAKERS (CHOOSE ONE)

1. There are many stories of famous people who achieved great goals through self-discipline. Who is your favorite example and why?

2. What is your definition of the word *discipline?*

GROUP DISCOVERY QUESTIONS

1. What did Paul mean when he wrote, "Work out your own salvation with fear and trembling"?

2. What is the relationship between faith and good works in regard to salvation?

3. What does the author say is the secret to godliness?

4. What is the relationship between the Christian working out his own salvation and God working in the Christian?

5. How are we to be different from the world?

6. How can we let people know what is going on in our lives and get prayer and support when we need it, without complaining? What is the difference between murmuring and disagreeing?

7. What are the disciplines of the Christian life? What are the advantages of being disciplined in following Christ? Is it possible to be too disciplined?

PERSONAL APPLICATION QUESTIONS

1. Are your feelings about the word *discipline* negative or positive? Why?

2. Do you think you are a disciplined person? Why or why not?

3. Which disciplines of the Christian life do you practice? Is there a discipline you would like to begin practicing in order to realize the full potential of all that you are and have in Christ?

4. Sometimes we spend so much effort trying to figure out what God wants that we forget to do the things we *know* God wants of us. According to the author, "When we are obedient to do all that we know God wants of us, then we have the joy of entering into all that God is doing in us." Are you obedient to all that you know God wants of you? If not, how can you change that?

5. If you were on trial for being a Christian, would you be convicted? On what basis?

6. In what ways do you shine as a light in the world?

7. If "the disciplines of the Christian life were never meant to be easy," how can we succeed?

OPTIONAL ACTIVITIES

1. Write down Bob Knight's definition of *discipline* and put it in a place you will see it often.

2. If you have decided to begin a new Christian discipline (or to be more regular in a discipline you now practice), make a note of it in your prayer box and pray for yourself in this endeavor.

PRAYER FOCUS

Thank God for doing His work in you and ask for His help in being obedient to do your part.

ASSIGNMENT

1. This week in your journal, write down how God is working in you and how you cooperate with Him.

2. Read through chapter 6 of the text and work through the corresponding study.

6 THE JOY OF MINISTRY
PHILIPPIANS 2:17–30
SESSION TOPIC

The three keys of effective ministry are selflessness, service, and suffering.

ICEBREAKERS (CHOOSE ONE)

1. Who was your role model as a child?

2. What is your ministry?

GROUP DISCOVERY QUESTIONS

1. Who are the role models for most American children today? What does that say about us as a nation? If you could choose role models for your own children, whom would you choose?

2. Paul's selfless service brought him joy. Does selflessness bring joy? Why or why not? Does selfishness bring sadness? If so, why is it so hard to let go of the self?

3. Why was Paul willing to sacrifice everything for the cause of Christ?

4. What did Paul sacrifice by sending Timothy and Epaphroditus to the Philippians? Why did he make this sacrifice?

5. Is it possible to escape the trap of selfishness in American society? How can the church help? Is the church itself ever caught in the trap? If so, in what ways?

6. How does one seek the good of Christ?

7. The author says one must learn to be a warrior as well as a worker in the ministry. If so, with whom are we fighting? Who, or what, are the rulers, authorities, and powers Paul wrote about in Ephesians 6:12? What are the characteristics of a good warrior?

PERSONAL APPLICATION QUESTIONS

1. Paul told the Philippians to follow him. Whom do you follow? Would you want anyone to follow you? Why or why not? Who does follow you?

2. Does suffering always come with discipleship? Why or why not? Have you ever suffered for the cause of Christ? If so, in what way?

3. When do you find it easy to put others first? When do you find it difficult to put others first? Should we always put others first?

4. Look at Philippians 1:21 and 2:21. Which verse best describes your life? Explain your answer.

5. Reread the author's quote of Bishop Ryle on pages 138 and 139. Are you a man or woman "of one thing"? Is it possible to be a man or woman "of one thing"?

OPTIONAL ACTIVITIES

1. When you go through your prayer box this week, pray for each person in his or her ministry.

2. Who has ministered to you through selflessness, service, or suffering? Write a letter or make a phone call thanking this person.

PRAYER FOCUS

Thank God that He calls us all to minister, and ask Him to give you an increased attitude of joy in your ministry.

ASSIGNMENT

1. This week, be aware of how Paul's example of selflessness, Timothy's example of service, or Epaphroditus's example of suffering can inspire you in your ministry. Make notes in your journal.

2. Read chapter 7 of the text and work through the corresponding study.

7 THE JOY OF HUMILITY
PHILIPPIANS 3:1–6
SESSION TOPIC
Rejoice only in Christ Jesus and not in who you are and what you have done.

ICEBREAKERS (CHOOSE ONE)
1. Describe a humble person. Describe a person who is not humble.

2. When Paul listed his own credentials in Philippians 3:4–6, he didn't sound very humble. Why, then, is this chapter titled "The Joy of Humility"?

GROUP DISCOVERY QUESTIONS
1. What were Paul's credentials? Do you think Paul could have accomplished all that he did if he had not been born with such advantages? Why or why not?

2. Would Paul's life have been considered a success by today's standards? Would Jesus's life? Why or why not?

3. What evidence do you see that Americans are obsessed with success? What type of success are we obsessed by? How is the American obsession with success antithetical to the gospel?

4. Why did it matter to Paul that some of the Philippian believers were being circumcised? Why was that so dangerous?

5. Give some examples of legalism in the church today. Who are the Judaizers of the church today?

6. What's dangerous about legalism? How does legalism destroy joy?

7. When do good works become legalism?

PERSONAL APPLICATION QUESTIONS

1. What are your credentials? How are they a benefit? How are they a stumbling block?

2. How do you feel about your frailties? Are you able to rejoice in your smallness?

3. Paul's zeal was striking, whether he was persecuting the church or furthering the cause of Christ. Are you zealous about anything? What inspires (or would inspire) zeal in you?

4. Are you ever legalistic? If so, in what ways?

5. Does legalism ever rob you of joy? Can you think of a time in your life when you experienced an abundance of joy?

6. The author gives the example of George Whitefield as a person who, in his early years, was very religious but was not a Christian. Are you counting on your good works to make you acceptable to God? What is the relationship between faith and works?

OPTIONAL ACTIVITIES

1. In your journal, write down the things you hope to accomplish before your death. Then answer the following questions:

a. Ultimately, will these accomplishments be the basis on which my life will be judged?

b. What will it mean to me if I am unable to achieve these goals?

2. Take the card with your name on it out of the prayer box. Write down the struggles you have with legalism. Pray for yourself in those struggles this week.

PRAYER FOCUS

Thank God that you can rejoice in Jesus Christ and do not have to depend on your own accomplishments.

ASSIGNMENT

1. In your prayer journal this week, write down any struggles you have with legalism and any moments of joy you experience.

2. Read chapter 8 of the text and work through the corresponding study.

8 THE JOY OF VICTORY
PHILIPPIANS 3:7–14
SESSION TOPIC

We cannot be victorious without paying the price.

ICEBREAKERS (CHOOSE ONE)

1. Who is your favorite athlete? What characteristics enable this person to be so successful in his or her field?

2. Name an achievement of yours that did not come naturally but was the result of much effort.

GROUP DISCOVERY QUESTIONS

1. What things do we sometimes see as assets that may actually be liabilities to the Christian?

2. Restate Matthew 16:25–26 in your own words. What does it mean to lose your life for Christ's sake?

3. What things did Paul count as useless in winning Christ?

4. One of Paul's goals was to know the Lord Jesus Christ. What does it mean to know Christ? How do we come to know Christ better?

5. Why did Paul want to know "the fellowship of His [Christ's] sufferings"? Did Paul speak of suffering as a positive or negative

experience? How does his view of suffering differ from that of our culture?

6. Is it possible to share in Christ's glory without sharing in His suffering? What is the difference between suffering and suffering for the sake of Christ?

7. What does the author give as a formula for success in the Christian life?

PERSONAL APPLICATION QUESTIONS

1. What do you do to grow in your knowledge of Christ? How intense is your striving to know Him?

2. Have you ever suffered for the cause of Christ? If so, in what way? If not, why do you think you have not?

3. One of the steps in the author's formula for success is to develop the discipline of maintaining one's focus. What distracts you as you strive to live out your faith?

4. Are you able to forget your failures, or do some failures continue to haunt you? How can you use your failures as opportunities for growth?

5. The author shares that a leader of the persecuted church once said that 95 percent of the believers who face the test of persecution

pass it, while 95 percent of the believers who face the test of prosperity fail it. Have you faced either the test of persecution or the test of prosperity? If so, how did you respond?

6. What is the cost of being faithful to the call of Christ? In what ways have you struggled with the cost of following Christ in your own life?

OPTIONAL ACTIVITIES

1. Do a topical study on the word *suffer* in the New Testament by using your concordance and cross-references. (Be sure to include Matthew 5:10–12 and Philippians 1:29 in your study.)

2. Go through the names of the people listed in your prayer box. Pray for them to be victorious in being faithful to the call of Christ. Pray for anyone who may be suffering.

PRAYER FOCUS

Thank God for calling you to follow Christ. Ask Him to give you intensity in your commitment.

ASSIGNMENT

1. Memorize Matthew 16:25–26. Meditate on those verses in your prayer time. Write down any thoughts you have in your prayer journal.

2. Read chapter 9 of the text and work through the corresponding study.

9 THE JOY OF MATURITY
PHILIPPIANS 3:15–21
SESSION TOPIC

We mature as Christians through encouragement, examples, personal purity, and the expectation of heaven.

ICEBREAKERS (CHOOSE ONE)

1. What is your definition of Christian maturity?

2. We've all heard children talk about what they would like to be or do when they grow up. Who do you hope to become as you strive toward Christian maturity?

GROUP DISCOVERY QUESTIONS

1. Is maturity necessarily a factor of age? Why or why not? If not, what does bring maturity?

2. Paul exhorted the Philippians to follow his example and the examples of other mature believers. Who can we pattern our lives after today? What kinds of people does our society present as role models?

3. How did Paul's view of the body differ from the Greeks of his day? Why was this difference significant?

4. What are the privileges and duties of a person's national citizenship? What are our privileges and duties as citizens of heaven?

5. How does our heavenly citizenship affect how we respond as citizens of our nation? Does our allegiance to our country ever conflict with our allegiance to heaven? Is nationalism a sin or a virtue?

6. What do believers need in order to keep pressing toward the goal of spiritual maturity? What, if anything, could keep a person from growing?

PERSONAL APPLICATION QUESTIONS

1. What does it mean to set your mind on earthly things or on heavenly things? In what ways do you struggle with keeping your mind on heaven?

2. What is one way you have become more mature in the last couple of years? What do you think contributed to this change?

3. The author quotes Malcolm Muggeridge as saying, "When I look back on my life nowadays,… what seemed at the time most significant and seductive, seems now most futile and absurd." What in your life seems significant now that may later prove to be unimportant? What will have lasting importance?

4. Has there ever been someone whose godly example you tried to imitate? If so, who? Who would be a good role model for you now?

5. In what ways does the expectation of Christ's return encourage you?

6. How have you seen God's transformation in your life?

7. Are you striving for spiritual maturity? If so, what things impede your progress? What encourages your progress?

OPTIONAL ACTIVITIES

1. Draw a graph of your spiritual development, showing both the times that you've grown and the dry times. Identify the circumstances that encouraged or impeded your growth.

2. Select from your prayer box the card of a person who has been a godly example to you. Pray for this person every day this week.

PRAYER FOCUS

Thank God that He works for our maturity. Ask Him to give you endurance and persistence for your spiritual climb.

ASSIGNMENT

1. This week in your prayer journal record the times when someone is a godly example to you. Also record the times when you may have been an example to someone else.

2. Read chapter 10 of the text and work through the corresponding study.

10 THE JOY OF HARMONY
PHILIPPIANS 4:1–5
SESSION TOPIC

We must do what we can to promote harmony in the body of Christ.

ICEBREAKERS (CHOOSE ONE)

1. Where do most people look for happiness?

2. Why does happiness seem so elusive?

GROUP DISCOVERY QUESTIONS

1. Why did Paul urge the Philippians to "stand fast in the Lord" rather than to march forward into battle?

2. Have you ever witnessed or been involved in a major church argument? If so, what was the argument about? What were the results?

3. Why are harmony and teamwork in the church important? Why was it so important to Paul that Euodia and Syntyche work out their differences?

4. What is the difference between joy and happiness? How is it possible to experience joy in negative circumstances? How is Paul an example of this?

5. How is pain connected to joy? How does our culture reinforce our avoidance of pain?

6. What did Paul mean when he wrote, "The Lord is at hand"? (Look up verse 5 in several translations.) Why would Paul have given this reminder to the Philippians? What effect should this reminder have on our behavior?

7. What is the importance of the ministry of reconciliation? Have you seen this ministry in your church? How can we all be reconcilers?

PERSONAL APPLICATION QUESTIONS

1. Read the prescription for unhappiness in the introduction to this chapter. Are any of these ten ideas true of you? If so, which ones? What could you do to change this?

2. In what ways do you avoid pain? Is this always to your benefit? Why or why not?

3. What did William Hendriksen mean by "big-heartedness"? In what ways are you big-hearted? In what ways are you defensive?

4. What does it mean to "rejoice in the Lord always"? What can you rejoice over?

5. What does it mean to let your gentleness (or moderation) be evident to all? How can you put verse 5 into practice?

6. What are Judson Edwards's six axioms for getting along with each other? Which of these rules are easy for you to follow, and which are more difficult?

OPTIONAL ACTIVITIES

1. Make a note in your prayer box to pray every day this week for harmony in the church.

2. Do a study on the important role of women in church history.

PRAYER FOCUS

Thank God for giving you reason to rejoice. Ask God to give you a spirit of "big-heartedness."

ASSIGNMENT

1. In your prayer journal, write down one or two of the ideas from the prescription for unhappiness that give you the most trouble. Record in your journal every time you do *not* give in to that philosophy.

2. Read chapter 11 of the text and work through the corresponding study.

11 THE JOY OF SECURITY
PHILIPPIANS 4:6–9
SESSION TOPIC
We can be freed from anxiety through prayer. Proper thoughts and actions will help us to continue in peace.

ICEBREAKERS (CHOOSE ONE)
1. What are the kinds of things that most people worry about?

2. Compared to most Americans, do you live in a high-stress or low-stress environment? What makes it high or low stress? Is there anything we can do about the stress in our lives?

GROUP DISCOVERY QUESTIONS
1. According to the author, only 8 percent of our worries have their basis in reality. Do you agree? Why or why not?

2. What physical, spiritual, and emotional harm can come from worry?

3. Is it always wrong to worry? Can anything beneficial come from worrying? If so, what?

4. What is the value of prayer when we are in a stressful or difficult situation?

5. What are Paul's six guidelines for proper meditation and thought? How can an understanding of these guidelines affect what we watch, listen to, and read?

6. What is the connection between thoughts and actions? Why is it important for us to control our thoughts?

PERSONAL APPLICATION QUESTIONS

1. To what fears and anxieties are you prone? How can Philippians 4:6–9 be a source of encouragement to you?

2. Share about a time when you prayed and got what you wanted. Share about a time when you prayed and did not get what you wanted. What made the difference?

3. How have you benefited from prayer, even when prayer did not change your situation?

4. What is the importance of thanksgiving in prayer? How much of your prayer life includes giving thanks?

5. Have you ever been in a difficult situation in which you experienced "the peace of God, which surpasses all understanding"? Explain.

6. What are you allowing into your thoughts that should not be there? What is the result of this wrong thinking? What could you replace these thoughts with that fits Paul's six guidelines?

OPTIONAL ACTIVITIES

1. Look up the following verses.

> Psalm 27:1–4
> Isaiah 26:3
> Isaiah 55:10–12
> John 14:27
> John 16:33

2. Pray for peace for yourself and for those whose names are in your prayer box.

PRAYER FOCUS

Pray to God about any anxieties that are currently on your mind. Thank Him for His gift of peace.

ASSIGNMENT

1. Memorize Philippians 4:6–9 or one of the verses listed under OPTIONAL ACTIVITIES. Record your reflections on this passage in your prayer journal.

2. Read chapter 12 of the text and work through the corresponding study.

12 THE JOY OF SERENITY
PHILIPPIANS 4:10–23
SESSION TOPIC

We, like Paul, can learn contentment.

ICEBREAKERS (CHOOSE ONE)

1. Which was your favorite chapter in this book? Why?

2. Where do people most often look for contentment?

GROUP DISCOVERY QUESTIONS

1. What is your definition of the well-lived life?

2. What was the secret of Paul's contentment? How can we learn to be content?

3. Do you agree that it can actually be harder to find contentment in times of abundance than in times of adversity? Why or why not? Give examples to support your opinion.

4. Read 1 Timothy 6:6–10. What is the danger of money? In what ways does the relative wealth of Christians in the United States confront us with a danger not faced by Christians in less affluent countries?

5. To whom does giving bring a blessing? How can this knowledge encourage us to be more generous in our giving? Is it a proper motive to give in order to receive blessing?

6. How important to Paul's contentment was the presence of supportive friends? Is it possible to be content without people around to support you?

7. What did Paul mean when he told the Philippians that God would supply all their needs? Can we claim that promise for ourselves? How do you explain Christians who have unmet needs for food, clothing, or shelter?

PERSONAL APPLICATION QUESTIONS

1. Is there anything that you want *more* of? If so, does that desire keep you from being content?

2. What were your feelings as you read the poem at the beginning of this chapter? Are you satisfied with where you are? What are the good things about where you are now?

3. Was there a time in your life when the power of God enabled you to be content in a difficult circumstance? If so, when? How do you draw strength from Christ?

4. Who are the people who support you? To whom are you a support? If you need a support group, make a commitment to begin building a support network this week.

5. Do you feel you are generous in your giving? Why or why not? Have you ever given sacrificially? Have you ever been the recipient of sacrificial giving?

6. What is the most important thing you have learned from this book? How will your life be different because of what you have learned?

OPTIONAL ACTIVITIES

1. Continue with your prayer box, making additions as needed.

2. Seek out an opportunity to give something to someone in need.

PRAYER FOCUS

Thank God that contentment is not dependent upon circumstances. Ask God to help you learn the secret of contentment.

ASSIGNMENT

1. This week in your prayer journal explore your struggles with contentment.

2. If the prayer journal has been helpful to you, continue to use it.

NOTES

CHAPTER 1

1. Howard E. Ferguson, *The Edge* (Cleveland: Getting the Edge Co., 1983), 1:25.

2. Dr. John Townsend, *Hiding from Love* (Grand Rapids, MI: Zondervan, 1991), 66–67.

3. Frank L. Houghton, *Amy Carmichael of Dohnavur* (London: Hodder & Stoughton, 1974), 250.

4. J. I. Packer, *God's Words* (Downers Grove, IL: InterVarsity Press, 1981), 193.

5. J. A. Motyer, *The Message of Philippians* (Downers Grove, IL: InterVarsity Press, 1984), 40.

6. Alva J. McClain, quoted in David L. Hocking, *How to Be Happy in Difficult Situations* (Winona Lake, IN: Brethren Missionary Herald, 1975), 24.

7. Judson Edwards, *What They Never Told Us about How to Get Along with Each Other* (Eugene, OR: Harvest House, 1991), 79–80.

8. Marian Evans, quoted in Alan Loy McGinnis, *The Friendship Factor*, rev. ed. (Minneapolis: Augsburg Fortress Publishers, 2004), 46.

9. C. S. Lewis, *Mere Christianity* (London: Fontana, 1952), 113–14.

10. Viktor Frankl, quoted in McGinnis, *The Friendship Factor*, 222–23.

CHAPTER 2

1. Dave Dravecky with Tim Stafford, *Comeback* (Grand Rapids, MI: Zondervan, 1990), 16.

2. Dravecky and Stafford, *Comeback*, 196–97.

3. Charles Colson, *Loving God* (Grand Rapids, MI: Zondervan, 1983), 248.

4. Warren W. Wiersbe, *Be Joyful* (Wheaton, IL: Victor Books, 1974), 37.

5. J. A. Motyer, *The Message of Philippians* (Downers Grove, IL: InterVarsity Press, 1984), 65.

6. Corrie ten Boom, *A Prisoner and Yet* (London: Christian Literature Crusade, 1954).

7. Clebe McClary with Diane Barker, *Living Proof* (Pawleys Island, SC: Clebe McClary, 1978), 40.

8. Paul S. Rees, *The Epistles to the Philippians, Colossians and Philemon* (Grand Rapids, MI: Baker, 1964), 31.

9. Anthony Robbins, *Awaken the Giant Within* (New York: Summit Books, 1991), 76–77.

10. William James, quoted in Charles Garfield, *Peak Performers* (New York: William Morrow and Company, 1986), 28.

11. David Jacobsen, "Remember Them," *Guideposts*, March 1991.

12. Jacobsen, "Remember Them."

13. Guy H. King, *Joy Way* (London: Marshall, Morgan & Scott, 1952), 33–34.

14. Paul S. Rees, *The Adequate Man* (Westwood, NJ: Revell, 1959), 30.

15. Howard E. Ferguson, *The Edge* (Cleveland: Getting the Edge Co., 1983), 1:9.

16. Motyer, *The Message of Philippians*, 72.

17. H. C. G. Moule, *Philippian Studies* (London: Hodder and Stoughton, 1897), 71.

18. William Hendriksen, *New Testament Commentary: Exposition of Philippians* (Grand Rapids, MI: Baker, 1979), 78.

19. Ralph A. Herring, *Studies in Philippians* (Nashville: Broadman, 1952), 53–54.

CHAPTER 3

1. John Stuart Mill, quoted in David Jeremiah, *Before It's Too Late* (Nashville: Thomas Nelson, 1982), 149.

2. Charles Colson, *Against the Night* (Ann Arbor, MI: Servant, 1989), 32–33.

3. *Epistle to Diognetus*, Chapter V, 4–11.

4. Warren W. Wiersbe, *The Integrity Crisis* (Nashville: Thomas Nelson, 1988), 17.

5. Sheldon Vanauken, *A Severe Mercy* (San Francisco: Harper & Row, 1977), 85.

6. Winston Churchill, quoted in Alan Loy McGinnis, *Confidence: How to Succeed at Being Yourself* (Minneapolis: Augsburg Fortress Publishers, 1987), 100.

7. Rudyard Kipling, *Verse* (Garden City, NY: Doubleday, Doranand Co., 1944), 559.

8. Tacitus, *Annals and Histories*, new ed. (New York: Alfred A. Knopf, 2009), 353–54.

9. E. H. Broadbent, *The Pilgrim Church* (London: Pickering and Inglis, Ltd., 1955), 124–25.

10. Anthony T. Padovano, *The Human Journey* (Garden City, NY: Doubleday, 1982).

11. Josef Tson, "Thank You for the Beating," *Christian Herald*, April 1988, 28–32.

12. James S. Hewett, ed., *Illustrations Unlimited* (Wheaton, IL: Tyndale, 1988), 19–20.

13. Winston Churchill, quoted in Alan Loy McGinnis, *Bringing Out the Best in People* (Minneapolis: Augsburg Fortress Publishers, 1985), 17–18.

CHAPTER 4

1. Alan Loy McGinnis, *The Power of Optimism* (San Francisco: Harper & Row, 1990), 15–16.

2. J. A. Motyer, *The Message of Philippians* (Downers Grove, IL: InterVarsity Press, 1984), 102.

3. Carroll E. Simcox, *They Met at Philippi* (New York: Oxford University Press, 1958), 67.

4. William Hendriksen, *New Testament Commentary: Exposition of Philippians* (Grand Rapids, MI: Baker, 1979), 98.

5. A. T. Robertson, *Word Pictures in the New Testament*, vol. 4 (Nashville: Broadman Press, 1930), 443.

6. J. Oswald Sanders, *Spiritual Leadership* (Chicago: Moody Press, 1967), 142.

7. Gary Inrig, *Quality Friendship* (Chicago: Moody Press, 1981), 166–67.

8. Peter F. Drucker, *The Effective Executive* (New York: HarperCollins, 1967), 53.

9. Paul C. Vitz, *Psychology as Religion* (Grand Rapids, MI: Eerdmans, 1995), 126.

10. F. B. Meyer, *The Epistle to the Philippians* (London: The Religious Tract Society, 1921), 81.

11. Paul S. Rees, *The Adequate Man* (Westwood, NJ: Revell, 1959), 43.

12. Dr. Robert Gromacki, *Stand United in Joy* (Grand Rapids, MI: Baker, 1980), 94.

13. Robertson, *Word Pictures*, 144.

14. C. S. Lewis, *Mere Christianity* (New York: Collier Books, 1952), 154–55.

15. Hendriksen, *Exposition of Philippians*, 112–13.

CHAPTER 5

1. Bob Knight, quoted in Howard E. Ferguson, *The Edge* (Cleveland: Getting the Edge Co., 1983), 3:12.

2. Forrest Gregg, quoted in Ferguson, *The Edge*, 3:12.

3. Tom Landry, quoted in Ferguson, *The Edge*, 3:13.

4. R. Kent Hughes, *Disciplines of a Godly Man*, rev. ed. (Wheaton, IL: Crossway, 2001), 12.

5. *Merriam-Webster's Collegiate Dictionary*, 11th ed., s.v. "discipline."

6. H. C. G. Moule, *Philippian Studies* (London: Hodder and Stoughton, 1897).

7. J. C. Ryle, *Holiness* (London: James Clarke & Co., 1952), viii.

8. Jerry Bridges, *The Practice of Godliness*, rev. ed. (Colorado Springs: NavPress, 1996), 33.

9. Jay E. Adams, *Godliness through Discipline* (Grand Rapids, MI: Baker, 1973), 3.

10. William Hendriksen, *New Testament Commentary: Exposition of Philippians* (Grand Rapids, MI: Baker, 1979), 120.

11. Kenneth S. Wuest, *Philippians in the Greek New Testament* (Grand Rapids, MI: Eerdmans, 1942), 75.

12. F. B. Meyer, *Devotional Commentary on Philippians* (Grand Rapids, MI: Kregel, 1979), 110.

13. J. Dwight Pentecost, *The Joy of Living* (Grand Rapids, MI: Kregel, 1973), 94.

14. Hughes, *Disciplines of a Godly Man*, 115.

15. Marc Peyser, "A Cheater's Guide to High Marks and Big $," *Newsweek*, January 6, 1992, 45.

16. J. A. Motyer, *The Message of Philippians* (Downers Grove, IL: InterVarsity Press, 1984), 133.

17. John D. Woodbridge, ed., *Great Leaders of the Christian Church* (Chicago: Moody Press, 1988), 281.

18. Clarence H. Faust and Thomas H. Johnson, eds., *Jonathan Edwards— Representative Selections, with Introduction, Bibliography, and Notes* (New York: Hill and Wang, 1962), 38.

CHAPTER 6

1. David J. Michell, "I Remember Eric Liddell," in Eric Liddell, *The Disciplines of the Christian Life* (Nashville: Abingdon, 1985), 14.

2. Randy Alcorn, *Christians in the Wake of the Sexual Revolution* (Sisters, OR: Multnomah, 1985), 153–54.

3. J. Oswald Sanders, *Paul the Leader* (Colorado Springs: NavPress, 1984), 8.

4. Warren W. Wiersbe, *The Integrity Crisis* (Nashville: Thomas Nelson, 1988), 40.

5. Sanders, *Paul the Leader*, 9.

6. J. Oswald Sanders, *Spiritual Leadership* (Chicago: Moody Press, 1967), 138–39.

7. William MacDonald, *True Discipleship* (Kansas City: Walterick Publishers, 1975), 30.

8. William Hendriksen, *New Testament Commentary: Exposition of Philippians* (Grand Rapids, MI: Baker, 1979), 134.

9. J. Dwight Pentecost, *The Joy of Living* (Grand Rapids, MI: Kregel, 1973), 109.

10. J. B. Lightfoot, *Saint Paul's Epistle to the Philippians* (Grand Rapids, MI: Zondervan, 1956), 123.

11. H. A. Ironside, *Notes on Philippians* (Neptune, NJ: Loizeaux Bros., 1922), 65.

12. J. C. Ryle, *Practical Religion* (London: James Clarke & Co., 1959), 130.

13. David J. Michell, in Liddell, *The Disciplines of the Christian Life*, 14–15.

CHAPTER 7

1. Geoffrey C. Ward, *Success Magazine*, April 1985, 55–56, quoted in Ted W. Engstrom with Robert C. Larson, *A Time for Commitment* (Grand Rapids, MI: Zondervan, 1987), 20–21.

2. F. B. Meyer, *Devotional Commentary on Philippians* (Grand Rapids, MI: Kregel, 1979), 144–45.

3. S. Lewis Johnson, "The Paralysis of Legalism," *Bibliotheca Sacra*, April–June 1963, 109.

4. Tim Hansel, *When I Relax, I Feel Guilty* (Colorado Springs: David C Cook, 1981), 43.

5. J. Oswald Sanders, *Paul the Leader* (Colorado Springs: NavPress, 1984), 8.

6. F. B. Meyer, *Paul* (Fort Washington, PA: Christian Literature Crusade, 1978), 17.

7. Sanders, *Paul the Leader*, 17.

8. George Whitefield, quoted in Bill Freeman, ed., *How They Found Christ: In Their Own Words* (Scottsdale, AZ: Ministry of the Word, 1983), 19–23.

CHAPTER 8

1. Vince Lombardi, quoted in Howard E. Ferguson, *The Edge* (Cleveland: Getting the Edge Co., 1983), 5:9.

2. Clarence E. Macartney, *The Greatest Men of the Bible* (New York: Abingdon, 1941), 14.

3. H. A. Ironside, *Notes on Philippians* (Neptune, NJ: Loizeaux Bros., 1922), 79–80.

4. Gordon Verrell, "Hershiser Closer to History," *Long Beach Press-Telegram*, September 25, 1988, C5, cited by Richard Mayhue, *Spiritual Intimacy* (Wheaton, IL: Victor Books, 1990).

5. William Hendriksen, *New Testament Commentary: Exposition of Philippians* (Grand Rapids, MI: Baker, 1979), 167–68.

6. Vince Lombardi, quoted in Ferguson, *The Edge*, 5:1.

CHAPTER 9

1. J. Oswald Sanders, *Paul the Leader* (Colorado Springs: NavPress, 1984), 46.

2. Guy H. King, *Joy Way* (London: Marshall, Morgan & Scott, 1952), 90–91.

3. C. S. Lewis, *Mere Christianity* (New York: Collier Books, 1952), 172.

4. H. Robert Cowles, "Secret Weapon in the Classroom," *The Word and Work*, August 1971, 229.

5. Lehman Strauss, *Devotional Studies in Philippians* (Neptune, NJ: Loizeaux Bros, 1959), 207.

6. Malcolm Muggeridge, *A Twentieth Century Testimony* (Nashville: Thomas Nelson, 1978).

7. Stephen R. Covey, The *Seven Habits of Highly Effective People* (New York: Simon and Schuster, 1989), 96.

8. Ralph A. Herring, *Studies in Philippians* (Nashville: Broadman, 1952), 92.

9. Edith Schaeffer, quoted in Louis Gifford Parkhurst Jr., *Francis Schaeffer: The Man and His Message* (Wheaton, IL: Tyndale, 1985), 115–16.

10. William Hendriksen, *New Testament Commentary: Exposition of Philippians* (Grand Rapids, MI: Baker, 1979), 184.

11. Author unknown.

12. J. A. Motyer, *The Message of Philippians* (Downers Grove, IL: InterVarsity Press, 1984), 197.

13. James Montgomery Boice, *Philippians: An Expositional Commentary* (Grand Rapids, MI: Baker, 1971, 2000), 223–24.

CHAPTER 10

1. James S. Hewett, ed., *Illustrations Unlimited* (Wheaton, IL: Tyndale, 1988), 281.

2. Watchman Nee, *Sit, Walk, Stand* (Fort Washington, PA: Christian Literature Crusade, 1957), 43–44.

3. Guy H. King, *Joy Way* (London: Marshall, Morgan & Scott, 1952), 90–91.

4. C. S. Lewis, *The Great Divorce* (New York: Macmillan, 1970), 18.

5. William Hendriksen, *New Testament Commentary: Exposition of Philippians* (Grand Rapids, MI: Baker, 1979), 191.

6. Dr. David Jeremiah with C. C. Carlson, *Escape the Coming Night* (Dallas: Word, 1990), 218.

7. J. A. Motyer, *The Message of Philippians* (Downers Grove, IL: InterVarsity Press, 1984), 201.

8. William Peter King, *The Search for Happiness* (New York: Abingdon, 1946), 9.

9. Lewis B. Smedes, *How Can It Be All Right When Everything Is All Wrong?* (New York: Harper & Row, 1982), 11, 52.

10. Clyde Reid, *Celebrate the Temporary* (New York: Harper & Row, 1972), 43–44.

11. Hendriksen, *Exposition of Philippians*, 193.

12. Judson Edwards, *What They Never Told Us about How to Get Along with Each Other* (Eugene, OR: Harvest House, 1991), 21–24.

13. Tim Hansel, *Holy Sweat* (Waco, TX: Word, 1987), 104–5.

CHAPTER 11

1. Tom Landry, quoted in Howard E. Ferguson, *The Edge* (Cleveland: Getting the Edge Co., 1983), 4:9.

2. Walter B. Knight, *Knight's Master Book of New Illustrations* (Grand Rapids, MI: Eerdmans, 1956), 755.

3. George Klingle, *The Golden West*, April 1919, 5.

4. "Talking to God: An Intimate Look at the Way We Pray," *Newsweek*, January 6, 1992, 39.

5. "Talking to God," *Newsweek*.

6. "Some Pray and Die," *HIS*, August 1944, 20–22, cited in W. Bingham Hunter, *The God Who Hears* (Downers Grove, IL: InterVarsity Press, 1986), 60–61.

7. J. A. Motyer, *The Message of Philippians* (Downers Grove, IL: InterVarsity Press, 1984), 211.

8. Norman B. Harrison, *His Peace: The Way of Living without Worrying* (Minneapolis: The Harrison Service, 1943), 14.

9. Maxwell Maltz, *Psycho-Cybernetics* (Englewood Cliffs, NJ: Prentice Hall, Inc., 1960).

10. J. H. Jowett, *The High Calling* (New York: Revell, 1909), 203.

11. Warren W. Wiersbe, *Be Joyful* (Wheaton, IL: Victor Books, 1974).

12. R. Kent Hughes, *Disciplines of a Godly Man*, rev. ed. (Wheaton, IL: Crossway, 2001), 72–73.

13. Viktor E. Frankl, *Man's Search for Meaning* (New York: Washington Square Press, 1959), 103–5.

14. S. I. McMillen and David E. Stern, *None of These Diseases* (Westwood, NJ: Revell, 1963), 96.

15. Jac J. Müller, The New International Commentary on the New Testament: *The Epistles of Paul to the Philippians and to Philemon* (Grand Rapids, MI: Eerdmans, 1955), 142.

16. Harrison, *His Peace*, 10.

17. James S. Hewett, ed., *Illustrations Unlimited* (Wheaton, IL: Tyndale, 1988), 496.

CHAPTER 12

1. Laurence Shames, *The Hunger for More* (New York: Time Books, 1989), x.

2. Shames, *The Hunger for More*, 80.

3. Shames, *The Hunger for More*, x.

4. Quoted in Charles R. Swindoll, *Simple Faith* (Dallas: Word, 1991), 175–76.

5. Harold Kushner, *Who Needs God?* (New York: Summit Books, 1989), 96–97.

6. A. T. Robertson, *Paul's Joy in Christ* (Westwood, NJ: Revell, 1927), 251.

7. Charles D. Kelley, "The Miracle of Contentment," *Discipleship Journal*, no. 42 (1987): 29.

8. Thomas Carlyle, quoted in Randy Alcorn, *Money, Possessions, and Eternity*, rev. ed. (Wheaton, IL: Tyndale, 2003), 46.

9. Cited in Paul S. Rees, *The Adequate Man* (Westwood, NJ: Revell, 1959), 114.

10. J. A. Motyer, *The Message of Philippians* (Downers Grove, IL: InterVarsity Press, 1984), 218–19.

11. J. S. Stewart, *A Man in Christ* (London: Hodder & Stoughton, 1972), 197–98.

12. William Hendriksen, *New Testament Commentary: Exposition of Philippians* (Grand Rapids, MI: Baker, 1979), 112.

13. Motyer, *The Message of Philippians*, 216.

14. J. B. Lightfoot, *St. Paul's Epistle to the Philippians* (London: Macmillan and Co., 1913), 11.

15. F. B. Meyer, *Devotional Commentary on Philippians* (Grand Rapids, MI: Kregel, 1979), 249.

16. John Witmer, quoted in Amanda and Stephen Sorenson, eds., *Time with God: The New Testament for Busy People: A One Year Devotional* (Dallas: Word, 1991), 491.

17. Quoted in Paul Lee Tan, ed., *Encyclopedia of 7,700 Illustrations: Signs of the Times* (Rockville, MD: Assurance Publishers, 1979), 273.

COMMENTARIES

Boice, James Montgomery. *Philippians: An Expositional Commentary*. Grand Rapids: Baker, 1971, 2000.

Gromacki, Robert. *Stand United in Joy*. Grand Rapids: Baker, 1980.

Harrison, Norman B. *His in Joyous Experience*. Chicago: The Bible Institute Colportage Association, 1926.

Hendriksen, William. *New Testament Commentary: Exposition of Philippians*. Grand Rapids, MI: Baker, 1979.

Herring, Ralph A. *Studies in Philippians*. Nashville: Broadman, 1952.

Ironside, H. A. *Notes on Philippians*. Neptune, NJ: Loizeaux Brothers, 1922.

King, Guy H. *Joy Way*. London: Marshall, Morgan & Scott, 1952.

Laurin, Roy L. *Life Advances*. Chicago: Van Kampen, 1953.

Lightfoot, J. B. *St. Paul's Epistle to the Philippians*. London: Macmillan and Co., 1913.

Maclaren, Alexander. *Expositions of Holy Scripture.* London: Hodder and Stoughton, 2005.

Martin, Ralph P. *The Epistle of Paul to the Philippians.* Grand Rapids: Eerdmans, 1959.

Meyer, F. B. *The Epistle to the Philippians.* London: The Religious Tract Society, 1921.

Motyer, J. A. *The Message of Philippians.* Downers Grove, IL: InterVarsity Press, 1984.

Moule, H. C. G. *Philippian Studies.* London: Hodder and Stoughton, 1897.

Müller, Jac J. *The Epistles of Paul to the Philippians and to Philemon,* The New International Commentary on the New Testament. Grand Rapids, MI: Eerdmans, 1955.

Pentecost, J. Dwight. *The Joy of Living.* Grand Rapids, MI: Kregel, 1973.

Rees, Paul S. *The Adequate Man.* Westwood, NJ: Revell, 1959.

Rees, Paul S. *The Epistles to the Philippians, Colossians and Philemon.* Grand Rapids, MI: Baker, 1964.

Robertson, A. T. *Paul's Joy in Christ.* Westwood, NJ: Revell, 1927.

Strauss, Lehman. *Devotional Studies in Philippians.* Neptune, NJ: Loizeaux Bros., 1959.

Walvoord, John F. *Philippians: Triumph in Christ.* Chicago: Moody Press, 1971.

Wiersbe, Warren W. *Be Joyful.* Wheaton, IL: Victor Books, 1974.

Wuest, Kenneth S. Wuest's Word Studies: *Philippians in the Greek New Testament.* Grand Rapids, MI: Eerdmans, 1942.

ADDITIONAL BOOKS BY DR. DAVID JEREMIAH

What in the World Is Going On?

A *New York Times* bestseller. The Bible has much to say about the end times, yet it is hard to piece together all the information. That is why Dr. David Jeremiah has written a unique book that identifies the ten most essential clues to Bible prophecy.

Life Wide Open

Many of us are easily discouraged by busyness, boredom, mediocrity, and routine, and these perplexities give us the sense that something is missing from our lives—passion. In *Life Wide Open*, Dr. David Jeremiah opens our eyes to how we can live a life of hope and enthusiasm, allowing the power of passion to permeate our souls.

Captured by Grace

Encountering grace changes lives forever. Let Dr. David Jeremiah show you how the transforming mercy that captured songwriter John Newton and the apostle Paul can awaken within you a fresh experience of the God who loves you fearlessly and pursues you with abandon.

Signs of Life

Signs of Life will lead you on a journey to a fuller understanding of the marks that identify you as a Christian. Personal imprints can affect souls for eternity and help you become a person of influence who radiates relevancy, authenticity, generosity, and compassion every day—just as Jesus did.

What to Do When You Don't Know What to Do

In his study on the book of James, Dr. David Jeremiah shows readers that a life lived with focused devotion to God should make a genuine difference in the way a person lives. His book will help you tap into God's supernatural strength to meet the challenges of your life.

These books were created from a teaching series by Dr. David Jeremiah. Each series is also available with correlating study guides and CD audio albums.

STAY CONNECTED TO DR. DAVID JEREMIAH

Take advantage of two great—absolutely free—ways to let Dr. David Jeremiah give you spiritual direction every day.

Turning Points **Magazine and Devotional**

Receive Dr. David Jeremiah's monthly magazine, *Turning Points*, each month:

- Monthly study focus
- Forty-eight pages of life-changing reading
- Relevant articles
- Special features
- Humor section
- Family section
- Devotional readings for each day of the month
- Bible study resource offers
- Live event schedule
- Radio and television information

Today's Turning Point **E-Devotional**

Start your day off right! Find words of inspiration and spiritual motivation waiting for you on your computer every morning. You can receive a daily e-devotion communication from Dr. David Jeremiah that will strengthen your walk with God and encourage you to live the authentic Christian life.

Sign up for these two free services online at www.DavidJeremiah.org.